Come Holy Spirit

Also by Barbara Del Buono
When Two Become One
The Miracle In Marriage

Co-author with Attorney John Del Buono
Acknowledged A Man
Survivor of Assault in the YMCA

Come Holy Spirit

A Guide to Confirming Faith in the Roman Catholic Church

By Barbara Del Buono

The Ellingsworth Press, LLC

Published by:
The Ellingsworth Press, LLC
680 Main Street
Watertown, CT 06795
Telephone: 860 274-7151
Toll Free: 877 ELLPRES (355-7737)
Web site: www.ellpress.com
E-mail: ELLPRESS @AOL.COM

The paper used in this book meets the requirements of the American National Standard for Permanence of Paper for Printed Library Materials
Z39.48.1984

Publisher's Cataloging-in-publication
(Provided by Quality Books, Inc.)

Del Buono, Barbara
      Come Holy Spirit
      Del Buono.
  1st ed.
  p. cm.
  Includes index:
  ISBN: 0960569839

First Edition
Manufactured in the United States of America

This book is dedicated to
five very special men who came into my life.

Monsignor John Mason Connor,
my marvelous instructor in the faith,

Reverend Kenneth S. Fulton,
a priest who is a friend who visits his people,

C. Robert Ingram,
my godfather and excellent example in the faith,

John Angelo Del Buono,
my husband,
who exemplifies what it means to be a man,

and

John Nicholas Del Buono,
my son,
who taught me more about God
than all the words in this book could teach anyone.

All of them have profoundly affected
my religious faith for the good.

Come Holy Spirit

I believe in You
Send forth Your love.
My faith I confirm,
Send down Your dove.

Come, Holy Spirit
Into my soul.
Set me on fire,
Make heaven my goal.

Let me be a witness
That Christ is my King.
Let me pay homage
As His praises I sing.

I'll serve You in life
'Til I breathe my last breath.
I know You will welcome me
At the time of my death.

'Til then, I am yours,
To use as You will.
Please send Your Spirit,
My whole life to fill.

Barbara Del Buono

Table of Contents

My Baptism Picture

My First Holy Communion Picture

My Confirmation Picture

I, _____

was confirmed on _____

at the church of _____

in _____.

My Confirmation Picture

The (Arch)Bishop who confirmed me was

_____.

My sponsor was_____.

My CCD teacher was_____.

My_____
taught me at home.

My Special Confirmation Pictures

My Special Confiramtion Pictures

Come Holy Spirit

Introduction

$\mathcal{P}$ersons seeking the sacrament of Confirmation in the Roman Catholic Church need to know that they are entering this faith with the knowledge and beliefs to be able to sustain them and not fall away before the time for marriage comes. Nowadays this happens all to often when Catholics do not get a good foundation in the basic tenets of their faith.

Parents are, and should be, the primary teachers of their children. This is especially true regarding religious beliefs. Therefore, it is the responsibility of parents to spend time with their child teaching him or her about God and His Church. The advent of Confirmation is an ideal time for parents to conduct formal instruction in the faith in their home with their child. It should be done one-on-one. Parents (or just the father or mother or godparent or good Catholic friend) should sit down on a weekly basis and review the essentials of the faith with the person about to be confirmed.

This type of instruction will benefit the child and the parent in that both know that the person to be confirmed *had knowledge* of the faith and the consequences that necessarily follow when the promises made at Confirmation are not kept. If the confirmed Catholic chooses to disobey the Commandments or the laws of the Church thereafter, they can rightfully be reminded that they are not practicing the faith in which they chose to believe. This knowledge also reinforces the choice of a practicing Catholic not to participate in events in their life in which they are not living up to the promises made at Confirmation to God and His Church.

I suggest that for the two years prior to the date for the Confirmation ceremony, you set aside one hour each week to spend with the person to be confirmed. This hour should be mutually agreeable and it needs to be at a time when other distractions will not interfere. Therefore, Sunday afternoon or evening may be the best time. It is a wonderful way to keep the Sabbath holy. It will be far more rewarding than any television show.

Read to the person to be confirmed from this book and allow him or her to interrupt at any time to ask questions. Talk with each other about the answers. You may be surprised at what is on his or her mind. This is an excellent way to find out. Expect that some children will not want to do this but insist on it anyway. This is YOUR time with your child and it does not interfere with what they are learning in Confraternity of Christian Doctrine (CCD) class.

It is probable that you have been a member of the Catholic Church for years and you know how difficult it is for you to conduct your life based on this faith in the permissive world we live in today. Sinful lifestyles are flaunted before us everyday and we are expected to go along silently without a word of disagreement. If we do offer words of objection we may be ridiculed, harassed and embarrassed and told we are old-fashioned and not up-to-date with the times.

Now is the time to tell the person seeking Confirmation that not everything can be tolerated without violating the promises made with God at confirmation. This is the most excellent time to reinforce the fact that a particular lifestyle goes along with being confirmed in the Catholic Church. It is one in which God's laws and those of His

Church are the standard for living one's entire life. It is the standard outside of ourselves that keeps us on the path to holiness and the one in which others have a right to expect us to live, particularly a married partner.

By reviewing the essentials of the Catholic faith with the person to be confirmed, you may be surprised at the increase of grace in your life. There is nothing that can compare with the benefit to be gained in spending this kind of time with the person to be confirmed. It is probably the most important thing you will do for him or her in his or her life. Do not miss this valuable opportunity that is presented to you.

This book is designed so that it may be a life-long treasure for your child (or any person being confirmed). Extra pages have been added so that you may capture forever the precious moments in which your child met Christ when receiving the Sacraments of the Church — through photographs. It is a gift that your child will keep long after you are no longer with him or her.

May God bless you and your child as you go forth on this journey in search of the Holy Trinity; God, the Father, Jesus Christ, the Son, and the Holy Spirit.

Prologue

I AM WHO AM

But Moses said to God, 'Who am I that I should go to
Pharaoh and lead the Israelites out of Egypt?' He answered,

'I will be with you; and this shall be your proof that it is I who
have sent you: when you bring my people out of Egypt, you
will worship God on this very mountain.'

'But,' said Moses to God, 'when I go to the Israelites and say
to them, 'The God of your fathers has sent me to you,' if they
ask me, 'What is his name?' what am I to tell them?' God
replied,

'I am who am.' Then he added, 'This is what you shall tell the
Israelites: I AM sent me to you.' God spoke further to Moses,
'Thus shall you say to the Israelites: The LORD, the God of
your fathers, the God of Abraham, the God of Isaac, the God
of Jacob, has sent me to you.

This is my name forever;
this is my title for all generations.'

Exodus 3:11-15

It is important for you to know the history of God with
His People. This history is contained in the Books of the
Bible. It is still the best-selling book of all time. But it is
not an ordinary book. The Word in this Book LIVES and
was inspired by God. It is one of the means by which God
speaks to His People. This Bible is made up of two parts,
the Old Testament and the New Testament.

The Book of Genesis in the Old Testament contains the story of Creation. After God created man, He created a special Land for him in the Garden of Eden. This was the first attempt by God to have man worship Him as the ONE AND ONLY TRUE GOD. Adam was the first man so blessed and He gave Adam dominion over all the land and creatures He had created.

When God saw that it was not good for Adam to be alone, He created Eve out of Adam's body and gave her to him to be his wife and helpmate. He blessed this couple greatly and asked only one thing of them in return: That they worship and obey Him and Him alone as their God and Creator.

When Adam and Eve were tempted to disobey God, they did. Their punishment for this disobedience is related in Genesis 3:14-19:

Then the LORD God said to the serpent:
'Because you have done this, you shall be banned
from all the animals
and from all the wild creatures;
On your belly shall you crawl,
and dirt shall you eat
all the days of your life.
I will put enmity between you and the woman,
and between your offspring and hers;
He will strike at your head,
while you strike at his heel.'

To the woman he said:
'I will intensify the pangs of your childbearing;
in pain shall you bring forth children.
Yet your urge shall be for your husband
and he shall be your master.'

To the man he said:
'Because you listened to your wife and ate from the tree

of which I had forbidden you to eat,
'Cursed be the ground because of you!
In toil shall you eat its yield
all the days of your life.

Thorns and thistles shall it bring forth to you,
as you eat of the plants of the field.
By the sweat of your face
shall you get bread to eat,
Until you return to the ground,
from which you were taken;
For you are dirt,
and to dirt you shall return.'

All of their descendants would inherit this punishment as well. This is what is meant when we say there is a stain of original sin on our souls when each of us is born. We inherit, from Adam and Eve, the punishment God inflicted on them for their act of disobedience to Him. But God did not abandon them nor does He abandon us.

After the fall of Adam and Eve from God's grace, He continues to send His prophets to His people to tell them of His love for them and to warn them of the dangers of disobedience to His Word. He frequently uses very ordinary, weak, sinful men to carry His message to His people. They are not all faithful to Him even after receiving great blessings from Him.

God makes covenants with man over and over again to try to get them to realize that He is the ONE TRUE GOD and that they should not worship idols that they make for themselves. He wants them to realize that power comes from Him and not from objects made by men. This is a hard lesson for man to learn and over and over man fails after having been blessed greatly by God.

When man turns from God, He takes away His blessings, but never abandons man. There is always the ray of hope that God will restore His people and that they will worship Him alone.

The story of Noah and his tribe are a good example of God's love. When God became angry with man and destroyed the world by water, Noah and his family were saved to begin a new generation of people who would love and obey the ONE TRUE GOD. When men became so proud that they built a Tower of Babel, God took away their most precious gift, the ability to speak one language. With the power of the Holy Spirit alone, He does this.

Again, He shows His love and His desire to have a race of people who will worship Him alone when He makes a covenant with Abraham. Abraham obeys God's directives to take his kinsfolk from his father's house to a land that God will show them. He promises to make of them a great nation and to bless them. He even tells Abraham that He will bless those who bless him and that He will curse those who curse him. God tells Abraham that "all the communities of the earth shall find blessing in you." Abraham obeyed God even to the point of being willing to kill his own son because God directed him to.

The generations after Abraham, who formed the "People of God", are full of stories of leaders of men who loved God and obeyed Him and leaders of men who fell away and disobeyed Him. The generations of people who loved God and followed His commands were blessed, and those that did not were cursed.

Another great prophet arose after Abraham and his name was Moses. His life was an exceptional one even before he learned of the ONE TRUE GOD. The most remarkable thing about Moses is that he spoke directly with God. God appeared to him in the form of a burning bush and from that moment on Moses' life was dedicated to God.

It is through this man that God took His People out of the Land of Egypt where they were slaves and led them back to His Promised Land. It is through Moses that we have received the most remarkable set of laws ever written, the Ten Commandments.

From the time of Moses, until the time of the New Testament, there appear a number of prophets blessed by God to send His Word to His People. Isaiah, Jeremiah, Ezekiel, Daniel, Hosea and Jonah are but a few of these special men of God who prophesied to His People and told them of the need for repentance. The birth of a Messiah that God would send to atone for sins and re-open the gates of Heaven to mankind was foretold.

The prophet Jeremiah foretells of a New Covenant God will make with His people:

> The days are coming, says the LORD, when I will make a new covenant with the house of Israel and the house of Judah. It will not be like the covenant I made with their fathers the day I took them by the hand to lead them forth from the land of Egypt; for they broke my covenant, and I had to show myself their master, says the LORD.
>
> But this is the covenant which I will make with the House of Israel after those days, says the LORD. I will place my law within them, and write it upon their hearts; I will be their God and they shall be my people. No longer will they have need to teach their friends and kinsmen how to know the LORD. All, from the least to greatest, shall know me, says the LORD, for I will forgive their evildoing and remember their sin no more.
>
> Jeremiah 31:31-34

This then is the story of the Old Testament:

✝ That God wants man to know that He is their ONE TRUE GOD.

✝ That He will bless them with His Ten Commandments and write each of them on their hearts.

✝ That He sends His prophets to them to warn of the dangers of disobedience; and the blessings that will come from loving and adoring Him alone.

✝ That He promises to send them a Messiah to save them from their sins and to re-open the gates of Heaven to them.

The New Testament is the witness of Christ's apostles that He is who He claimed to be - the Son of God. He is the promised Messiah sent to save man from his sins and to re-open the gates of Heaven for man. He chose twelve very ordinary men to bring His message to His People. Only one of the twelve betrayed Him and that one committed suicide when he realized what he had done. Ten of these twelve were persecuted and killed for their witness that Jesus Christ is the Son of God and none of them ever recanted their belief that Christ is who He said He was. Only one, John, died of old age. He was the most beloved apostle of Christ and he was the only one at the foot of the cross as Christ died.

Before Christ's apostles died, they did as He had commanded them and established His Church on earth. While Christ lived He told his disciples to:

Baptize His people with water in the name of the Father, Son and Holy Spirit,

Feed His people with His Body and His Blood,

Forgive His people their sins,

Confirm His people in the faith so that the Holy Spirit would come to them,

Bless the marriages of His people,

Ordain the men He calls to be His apostles, to serve His people and

Anoint the sick among His people.

These are the seven sacraments of the Church that Christ left for us and there is no other place on earth to go and receive these gifts from God.

After Christ died on the cross for our sins, He arose from the dead and appeared on earth to His disciples. After His Resurrection He ate with them and stayed with them for forty days. After that some of His disciples were with Him when He ascended into Heaven and are witness to this awesome event.

This then is the message of the New Testament:

☦ That Jesus Christ is the Son of God.

☦ That He chose twelve men to be his apostles.

☦ That He established His church on earth through His apostles.

☦ That He left seven sacraments for His people to sustain them in their life on earth.

☦ That He died on a cross to atone for the sins of His people.

☦ That He arose from the dead.

☦ That He ascended into Heaven.

Now it is time to learn about this wonderful Church that Christ established for you.

To the Baptized Child of God

Confirmation in the Roman Catholic Church is the time when you are asked to confirm your faith in God because you choose to do so. You will be making many promises to God as you do this. It is the most important challenge you will face in your lifetime because the rest of your life depends on the answer to one question. Who is Christ?

Was He the Son of God? Is He really the promised Messiah? Is He going to be the authority in your life? Will you be able to live a life based on Christ's teachings? Are you willing to accept the Ten Commandments as the laws of God? Will you accept the laws of the Catholic Church with regard to the Sacraments? What kind of life will you be giving up if you make these promises?

You have met God in the sacraments of *Baptism*, *Confession* and *Holy Communion*. Ordinarily this will have happened to you as a child. But now you must stand apart from anyone else, including your parents, and decide whether or not you want to confirm your belief in Jesus Christ as the Son of God. If you say "yes" to confirmation, then you will be asking to receive the gift of the Holy Spirit in your life. He will come to bless you as you make this serious commitment.

If you take Confirmation seriously it will change your life for the better. All that God has planned for you to accomplish in your life will now have His power operating in everything you do. The power of the Holy Spirit will descend on you. He is the Third Person of the Holy Trinity and is the living, breathing LOVE that constantly flows from the Father to the Son and back to the Father. It is hard for us to imagine the POWER of this kind of love, but it is a love so great that the Father and the Son are ONE with the Holy Spirit.

The Old and New Testaments are full of descriptions of the power of the Holy Spirit. He comes to us in the form of wind, breath and fire. He is always breathing life into the Word of God. He is the way in which God takes ordinary, weak, sinful men and accomplishes marvelous deeds through them.

This same Holy Spirit will come to you if you make your Confirmation worthily. Remember: *Confirmation will mark your life as a Christian forever and your actions hereafter will give glory or scandal to Christ and His Church at all times. Your friendship with Him from now on will constantly lift Him and His Church up—or bring them down—depending on whether you follow His teachings as best you can.*

Prayers

$\mathcal{I}$f we are to worship God as our Father, then we need a way to talk with Him. Prayer is the language we use when speaking with Our Heavenly Father who we cannot see face to face. Our prayers with God should always begin with acts of praise and glory.

One of your first acts as a child was to learn how to pray. The prayers of children are very special to God and all parents who acknowledge the reality of God want their children to learn how to pray when they first learn to talk. A child as young as two years of age can learn to make the **Sign of the Cross** and say it before meals and at bed-time.

Prayer is like a light that shines between you and God. It can be said in private at any time. But there will be times when you gather together with other Catholics. When the Christian community comes together like this, it is for the purpose of prayer. Try to imagine that each member in the congregation is holding a candle and the only way to light that candle is by opening our hearts and then our mouths to pray together. If only a few do this there will be very little light shining between God and His people in His Church. On the other hand, if all of the people open their hearts and say these prayers meaningfully, then there will be a great light shining between God and His people in His Church.

Perhaps now you can begin to see that if you do not know these special prayers and use them, you will be hindering all of the other members of the Church because your light will not be shining among those who do know these prayers and use them. When you are asking for Confirmation of your faith, you are asking to become a child of the "light" not the darkness. Then you must let the "light" of your prayers shine any time you are at public worship.

The special prayers that you need to know are these:

The Sign of the Cross

The Lord's Prayer, or "Our Father"

The Hail Mary

The Act of Contrition

The Nicene Creed

The Glory Be

It would be easy to say that you should "know" them, but to know them is not enough. Knowing also includes understanding their meaning and significance. Prayer is the greatest weapon a Christian has in his every day battle against the forces of evil in his life. Only by knowing and understanding this weapon can you successfully use it against the temptations that will be thrust in front of you by the forces of evil.

THE SIGN OF THE CROSS

This is the universal prayer of the Church that can be understood by anyone, anywhere because it is said in sign language. People the world over recognize and understand its meaning by the sign you make when you say it.

This prayer is said by:

placing the fingers of the right hand on your forehead and saying, **IN THE NAME OF THE FATHER,**

then moving your hand to your chest and saying, **AND OF THE SON,**

then moving your hand to your left shoulder and saying, **AND OF THE HOLY,**

then moving your hand to your right shoulder and saying, **SPIRIT,**

and then folding your hands together and saying, **AMEN.**

Now you have prayed a significant prayer.

By this prayer you are affirming a belief in One God in Three Divine Persons. We use the word "mystery" in connection with this belief because this concept of Three Divine Persons being present in One God is something we cannot completely understand or explain with our limited humanity and it must be accepted with faith.

Socrates was a Greek who lived several centuries before Christ came to earth. He was a teacher and philosopher. Through his own reason he had come to the conclusion that there could only be **ONE GOD**. He was teaching the students of Athens to use their reason to come to the same belief. His fellow Greeks became so upset with him over this that they forced him to drink a poisonous cup of hemlock that took his life. The idea of only **ONE GOD** is still a dangerous belief to hold.

The Jewish people were the first witnesses as a community of people to the reality of only **ONE GOD** when everyone else in the known world believed in many gods. For this witness God blessed and protected them in very special ways. He called them **HIS CHOSEN PEOPLE.**

It was not easy for the Chosen People to live in a world where everyone else believed in many gods while they did not. They were often laughed at, ridiculed and even persecuted and killed for this belief.

You, too, live in a world where the idea of **ONE GOD** is often criticized and ridiculed. You must also realize that there are those in your world who claim there is **NO GOD**. Being confirmed in the Catholic faith will be a difficult life for you to lead but the Holy Trinity will be with you in all of the battles you must fight to assert your belief.

The prayer of the Sign of the Cross is a very significant one. It says to everyone that you believe in **ONE GOD, THE FATHER, THE SON, AND THE HOLY SPIRIT.**

God has not left you alone without any reason on which to base this belief. Besides the wonderful order in the universe, and in nature that you have the ability to observe for yourself, He has sent his prophets to tell us who He is. His Inspired Word has been recorded for all time for all people to read.

Through Isaiah, a prophet of the Old Testament, we know what God the Father has said of Himself.

> You are my witnesses, says the LORD,
> my servants whom I have chosen
> To know and believe in me
> and understand that it is I.
> Before me no god was formed,
> and after me there shall be none.
>
> It is I, I the LORD;
> there is no savior but me.
> It is I who foretold, I who saved;
> I made it known, not any strange god among you;
>
> You are my witnesses, says the LORD.

I am God, yes, from eternity I am He; There is none who can
deliver from my hand:
who can countermand what I do?

Isaiah 43:10-13

Thus says the LORD, Israel's King
and redeemer, the LORD of hosts;
I am the first and I am the last;
There is no God but me.

Isaiah 44:6

For thus says the LORD,
The creator of the heavens,
who is God,
The designer and maker of the earth
who established it,
Not creating it to be a waste,
but designing it to be lived in:
I am the LORD, and there is no other.
I have not spoken from hiding
nor from some dark place of the earth,
And I have not said to the
descendants of Jacob,
'Look for me in an empty waste.'
I, the LORD, promise justice,
I foretell what is right.

Isaiah 45:18,19

Turn to me and be safe,
all you ends of the earth,
for I am God; there is no other!

Isaiah 45:22

The prophet Isaiah also relates what God the Father has
said about the coming of the Redeemer, the Messiah,
Jesus Christ, the Son of God.

Therefore the Lord himself will give you this sign: the virgin
shall be with child, and bear a son, and shall name him
Immanuel.

Isaiah 7:14

For a child is born to us, a son is given us;
upon his shoulder dominion rests;
They name him Wonder-Counselor, God-Hero,
Father-Forever, Prince of Peace.

Isaiah 9:5

See, the Lord proclaims to the ends of the earth: Say to
daughter Zion, your savior comes!

Isaiah 62:11

Further, the prophet Isaiah described the Redeemer for
us so that when He comes we will be able to recognize
Him.

But a shoot shall sprout from the stump of Jesse,
and from his roots a bud shall blossom.
The spirit of the LORD shall rest upon him:
a spirit of wisdom and of understanding,
A spirit of counsel and of strength,
a spirit of knowledge and of fear of the LORD,
and his delight shall be the fear of the LORD.
Not by appearance shall he judge,
nor by hearsay shall he decide,
But he shall judge the poor with justice,
and decide aright for the land's afflicted.
He shall strike the ruthless with the rod of his mouth,
And with the breath of his lips he shall slay the wicked.
Justice shall be the band around his waist,
and faithfulness a belt upon his hips.

Isaiah 11:1-5

Therefore, thus says the Lord GOD:
See, I am laying a stone in Zion,
a stone that has been tested,
A precious cornerstone as a sure foundation;
he who puts his faith in it shall not be shaken.

Isaiah 28:16

It is foretold in the Book of Micah where Christ would be
born:

> But you, Bethlehem-Ephrathah,
> too small to be among the clans of Judah,
> From you shall come forth for me
> one who is to be ruler in Israel;
> Whose origin is from of old,
> from ancient times.

Micah 5:1

These are but a few of the passages from the Old Testament that reveal to us what God wants us to know of Him and His Son.

The New Testament is the witness of Christ's apostles and disciples that He lived; that He revealed to them the truth of who He is. Their witness is very important to you and to me living today. Each of these men was an ordinary person like you and me. Jesus chose each one of the apostles for this special mission. After Christ's Ascension all of these men went about the world teaching about Jesus and NONE of them denied Him, even in the face of death.

The New Testament Book of St. John was written for the purpose of being a witness to us that Jesus Christ is Divine, that He is the Son of God. St. John tells us this plainly in these words.

> But these have been recorded to help you believe that Jesus is the Messiah, the Son of God, so that through this faith you may have life in his name.

John 20:31

St. John was the youngest of the apostles. Christ loved John dearly for his devotion to him. John speaks to us clearly about the Divinity of Christ in Chapter 1 of the Prologue to his gospel.

> In the beginning was the Word;
> the Word was in God's presence,
> and the Word was God.

He was present to God in the beginning.
Through him all things came into being,
and apart from him nothing came to be.

Whatever came to be in him, found life,
life for the light of men.
The light shines on in darkness,
a darkness that did not overcome it.

There was a man named John sent by God, who came as
a witness to testify to the light, so that through him all men
might believe — but only to testify to the light, for he himself
was not the light. The real light which gives light to every man
was coming into the world.

He was in the world,
and through him the world was made,
yet the world did not know who he was.
To his own he came,
yet his own did not accept him.
Any who did accept him
he empowered to become children of God.

These are they who believe in his name—who were begotten
not by blood, nor by carnal desire, nor by man's willing it, but
by God.

The Word became flesh
and made his dwelling among us,
and we have seen his glory:
The glory of an only Son coming from the Father,
filled with enduring love.

John testified to him by proclaiming: 'This is he of whom
I said, "The one who comes after me ranks ahead of me,
for he was before me."
Of his fullness
we have all had a share –
love flowing upon love.

For while the law was given through Moses, this enduring love came through Jesus Christ. No one has ever seen God. It is God the only Son, ever at the Father's side, who has revealed him.

John 1:1-18

But Christ spoke of his own Divinity. When He was talking with the Samaritan woman at the well,

The woman said to him: 'I know there is a Messiah coming.' (This term means Anointed.) 'When he comes, he will tell us everything.' Jesus replied, 'I who speak to you am he.'

John 4:25,26

In a discourse with the Jews,

They cried, 'We are no illegitimate breed! We have but one father and that is God himself.' Jesus answered:

'Were God your father
you would love me,
for I came forth from God, and am here.
I did not come of my own will;
it was he who sent me.
Why do you not understand what I say?
It is because you cannot bear to hear my word.
The father you spring from is the devil,
and willingly you carry out his wishes.
He brought death to man from the beginning,
and has never based himself on truth;
the truth is not in him.
Lying speech
is his native tongue;
he is a liar and the father of lies.
But because I deal in the truth,
you give me no credence.
Can any one of you convict me of sin?
If I am telling the truth,
why do you not believe me?

Whoever is of God
hears every word God speaks.
The reason you do not hear
is that you are not of God.'

John 8:41-47

These are strong words from the mouth of Jesus. We had better heed them for to ignore them is to do so at our peril. Another time:

Jesus was walking in the temple area, in Solomon's Portico, when the Jews gathered around him and said, 'How long are you going to keep us in suspense? If you really are the Messiah, tell us so in plain words.' Jesus answered:
'I did tell you, but you do not believe.
The works I do in my Father's name
give witness in my favor,
but you refuse to believe
because you are not my sheep.
My sheep hear my voice.
I know them,
and they follow me.
I give them eternal life,
and they shall never perish.
No one can snatch them out of my hand.
My Father is greater than all, in what he has given me,
and there is no snatching out of his hand.
The Father and I are one.'

John 10:23-30

When Jesus did what the Jews had asked Him to do, speak plainly to them, they could not bear the light of truth that He was speaking and they fetched stones with which to stone Him. Jesus protested to them:

'Many good deeds have I shown you from the Father. For which of these do you stone me?'

John 10:32

'It is not for any "good deed" that we are stoning you,' the
Jews retorted, 'but for blaspheming. You who are only a man
are making yourself God.' Jesus answered:
'Is it not written in your law,
"I have said, You are gods"?
If it calls those men gods
to whom God's word was addressed –
and Scripture cannot lose its force –
do you claim that I blasphemed
when, as he whom the Father consecrated
and sent into the world,
I said, "I am God's Son"?
If I do not perform my Father's works,
put no faith in me.
But if I do perform them,
even though you put no faith in me,
put faith in these works,
so as to realize what it means
that the Father is in me
and I in him.'

John 10:33-38

Jesus is imploring us as well as the Jews in this Scripture,
to believe that He is the Son of God and can heal our
lives from sin just as He wanted to heal the lives of those
He was speaking to in this gospel. All men must answer
this question for themselves. "Who is Christ?"

Pontius Pilate, the Roman Governor of Judea, asked
Christ this question when He was before him for judg-
ment under the Roman law. "Are you the king of the
Jews?"

Jesus answered:
My kingdom does not belong to this world.
If my kingdom were of this world,
my subjects would be fighting
to save me from being handed over to the Jews.
As it is, my kingdom is not here.'

John 18:36

> At this Pilate said to him, 'So, then, you are a king?'
> Jesus replied:
> 'It is you who say I am a king.
> The reason I was born,
> the reason why I came into the world,
> is to testify to the truth.
> Anyone committed to the truth hears my voice.'

John 18: 37

Christ was put on trial before the Jewish Sanhedrin and the High Priest of the Sanhedrin, Caiaphas, also questioned Christ about His claim to Divinity:

> 'I order you to tell us under oath before the living God whether you are the Messiah, the Son of God.' Jesus answered: 'It is you who say it. But I tell you this: Soon you will see the Son of Man seated at the right hand of the Power and coming on the clouds of heaven.' At this the high priest tore his robes: 'He has blasphemed! What further need have we of witnesses? Remember, you heard the blasphemy. What is your verdict?' They answered, 'He deserves death!' Then they began to spit in his face and hit him. Others slapped him, saying: 'Play the prophet for us, Messiah! Who struck you?'

Matthew 26:63-68

We must all answer the question that Caiaphas asked. What is your verdict? Is Christ the Son of God or is He a blasphemer? Is He Divine or was He just a man? Jesus was put on trial for claiming that He was Divine. If we recognize His Divinity, we too will be put on trial. Jesus tells us clearly that He is the Messiah; that He has come from God; that we must believe in Him if we are to be saved from our sins.

The Gospels of Matthew, Mark, Luke and John are a witness to us that what Christ said is true. Each wrote about His being questioned about His Divinity and the fact that

- all have subscribed to His Divinity is for our benefit. St. Luke writes about Christ being questioned by Caiaphas:

> Once they had brought him before their council, they said, 'Tell us, are you the Messiah?' He replied, 'If I tell you, you will not believe me, and if I question you, you will not answer. This much only will I say: "From now on, the Son of Man will have his seat at the right hand of the Power of God." 'So you are the Son of God?' they asked in chorus. He answered, 'It is you who say I am.' They said, 'What need have we of witnesses? We have heard it from his own mouth.'
>
> Luke 22:66-71

St Mark also recorded this encounter for us.

> Once again the high priest interrogated him: 'Are you the Messiah, the Son of the Blessed One?' Then Jesus answered: 'I am; and you will see the Son of Man seated at the right hand of the Power and coming with the clouds of heaven.'
>
> Mark 14: 61,62

There is a Third Person of the Trinity that we are asked to believe in when we pray the prayer of the Sign of the Cross. It is the Holy Spirit. Jesus is witness that the Holy Spirit is **REAL**, and is necessary in our lives. This is what Jesus said of the Holy Spirit.

> Yet I tell you the sober truth:
> It is much better for you that I go.
> If I fail to go,
> the Paraclete will never come to you,
> whereas if I go,
> I will send him to you.
> When he comes,
> he will prove the world wrong
> about sin,
> about justice,
> about condemnation.
> About sin—

in that they refuse to believe in me;
about justice—
from the fact that I go to the Father
and you can see me no more;
about condemnation—
for the prince of the world has been condemned.
I have much more to tell you,
but you cannot bear it now.
When he comes, however,
being the Spirit of truth,
he will guide you to all truth.
He will not speak on his own,
but will speak only what he hears,
and will announce to you the things to come.
In doing this he will give glory to me,
because he will have received from me
what he will announce to you.
All that the Father has belongs to me.
That is why I said that what he will announce to you
he will have from me.

John 16: 7-15

You will receive power when the Holy Spirit comes down on you; then you are to be my witnesses in Jerusalem, throughout Judea and Samaria, yes, even to the ends of the earth.

Acts 1: 8

The revealed Word of God the Father, Jesus the Son and the Holy Spirit are direct and clear. We have been given every reason to believe that these words in the Scripture are true and are to be followed.

Therefore, the Sign of the Cross is a powerful prayer indeed. It is probably the shortest of all prayers and yet it encompasses the basic foundation of our faith. This simple prayer will be the one most uttered by you throughout your life and especially at the hour of your death. It was said at your baptism when you entered into this faith; it is said at the beginning of every Mass; and hopefully will be said by a priest at the time of your death.

THE LORD'S PRAYER
or OUR FATHER

The most special prayer to all Christians is this one. The apostles talked with Christ while He was on earth about how to pray. Christ's answer was the prayer, Our Father.

St. Matthew recorded Christ's dissertation on this prayer:

> When you are praying, do not behave like the hypocrites who love to stand and pray in synagogues or on street corners in order to be noticed. I give you my word, they are already repaid. Whenever you pray, go to your room, close your door, and pray to your Father in private. Then your Father, who sees what no man sees, will repay you.
> In your prayer do not rattle on like the pagans. They think they will win a hearing by the sheer multiplication of words. Do not imitate them. Your Father knows what you need before you ask him. This is how you are to pray:
>
> Our Father in heaven,
> hallowed be your name,
> your kingdom come,
> your will be done
> on earth as it is in heaven.
> Give us today our daily bread,
> and forgive us the wrong we have done
> as we forgive those who wrong us.
> Subject us not to the trial
> but deliver us from the evil one.
>
> If you forgive the faults of others, your heavenly Father will forgive you yours. If you do not forgive others, neither will your Father forgive you.
>
> *Matthew 6:5-15*

Our Father in heaven. Many people ask: "Is there really a heaven?" When Christ began to pray he addressed God as Father *in Heaven*. If you believe in Christ, you must believe in Heaven. And why not? Heaven is the place we all hope to attain after our death on earth. But there are many people who believe there is no life after this one. Christ tells us directly, in this prayer, that there is a heaven and it is the place where God dwells.

Hallowed be your name. Christ is teaching us that the name of God is a sacred one and we should always address Him in a reverent and respectful manner. The word "hallowed" means sacred.

Your kingdom come, Your will be done on earth as it is in heaven. God's kingdom is not a worldly one though it is in this world that we must live. However, there is a part of us that does not belong to this world and it is our spirit. Yet, while we are on earth we are very connected to the world and our spirit. Christ is King of our spiritual world and we invite Him into this kingdom that really belongs to him. We ask God for His will to be done in our life and we can be sure if we mean this that it will be free from sin. Sin does not exist in the kingdom of God

Give us today our daily bread. Whether we recognize it or not, we are dependent on God for our daily sustenance. The very air we breathe comes from Him and we would surely die without it. He showed His power to provide for His people when He led the Israelites out of the land of Egypt and fed their bodies with manna that He sent down from heaven. When Christ was on earth the matter of food came up on a mountainside where He was teaching thousands of people. With just a few loaves and fishes He fed them all! What further proof do we need that God provides our daily bread?

And forgive us the wrong we have done as we forgive those who wrong us. This is surely the most difficult prayer we shall ever pray. It imposes on us a duty that we do not want to face. It makes us realize our own wrongs (or debts or trespasses) and know that first we will have to forgive those who do wrongs to us before we can be forgiven our wrongs. What a difficult teaching this is to hear!

Subject us not to the trial but deliver us from the evil one. Do you believe the devil really exists? Many people do not believe in God or the devil, in heaven or in hell. This is the world in which you live and it is a place where the devil and the evil he does really exist. If you deny this, the devil already has a hold on you. Christ is teaching us in this prayer to pray to our heavenly Father for deliverance from the evil one. If you say this part of the prayer meaningfully, it will change the way you live your life.

Our Protestant friends add these words to this prayer:

FOR THINE IS THE KINGDOM, THE POWER AND THE GLORY, FOREVER, AMEN.

These words are added to the Mass at a different place than when we say the prayer, Our Father. There is an explanation for this. In the early days of Christianity, before the invention of the printing press, the Bible was copied and translated primarily by monks who devoted their lives to this work. One such monk became so fervent when copying this prayer that he added these words in the margin from his own heart. Another translator picked them up as being part of the original prayer and included them as the original words. That is why there is a difference in the Protestant version of this prayer and the Catholic version.

THE HAIL MARY

Hail Mary, full of grace. The beginning of this prayer is an exclamation of tribute to the most honored and powerful human being the world has ever known. Mary is the embodiment of the promise God made to us through Isaiah when He said:

Therefore the Lord himself will give you this sign: the virgin
shall be with child, and bear a son, and shall name him
Immanuel.

Isaiah 7:14

When God sent the angel Gabriel to Mary to tell her that
he had been sent from God to announce the conception
of Jesus in her virgin womb, she consented obediently,
though the dangers and risks to her were very great. In
those days the punishment for becoming pregnant
before marriage was public stoning to death. Although
she was betrothed to Joseph, they were not yet married
and she knew the risk she was taking in consenting to the
virgin birth of Jesus. **SHE** was the sign that God had
promised so that we would recognize the Messiah when
He would come. Only one who was as full of grace as
Mary could become the mother of Jesus.

The apostle, St. Luke, a physician, knew Mary and recorded these words for us about her.

Upon arriving, the angel said to her: 'Rejoice, O highly
favored daughter! The Lord is with you. Blessed are you
among women.' She was deeply troubled by his words, and
wondered what his greeting meant. The angel went on to say
to her: 'Do not fear, Mary. You have found favor with God.
You shall conceive and bear a son and give him the name
Jesus. Great will be his dignity and he will be called Son of
the Most High. The Lord God will give him the throne of David
his father. He will rule over the house of Jacob forever and
his reign will be without end.'
Mary said to the angel, 'How can this be since I do not know
man?' The angel answered her: 'The Holy Spirit will come
upon you and the power of the Most High will overshadow
you: hence, the holy offspring to be born will be called Son of
God. Know that Elizabeth your kinswoman has conceived a
son in her old age; she who was thought to be sterile is now
in her sixth month, for nothing is impossible with God.'
Mary said: 'I am the servant of the Lord. Let it be done to me
as you say.' With that the angel left her.

Luke 1:28-38

As Mary spoke these words she became a participant in the role of salvation by allowing God to use her for the birth of His Son among men. Without the use of modern technology, Mary knew that her baby would be a boy. She willingly gave her love, trust and obedience to God. Eve had this same opportunity but failed in her test of love. She was unable to willingly give her love, trust and obedience to God when Satan tempted her. All that was lost through Eve was restored through Mary. She is truly our most admirable model among all the saints.

The Lord is with you. Blessed are you among women and blessed is the fruit of your womb Jesus.

We choose with our lives which mother of mankind we **WILL** to follow. When our choice is Mary, we are affirming our belief that Christ is the Son of God. We are also recognizing that Mary is our mother, given to us by Christ at the foot of the Cross.

> Near the cross of Jesus there stood his mother, his mother's sister, Mary the wife of Clopas, and Mary Magdalene. Seeing his mother there with the disciple whom he loved, Jesus said to his mother, 'Woman, there is your son.' In turn he said to the disciple, 'There is your mother.' From that hour onward the disciple took her into his care.
>
> *John 19:25-27*

Through her intercession with her powerful and divine son, many graces may flow into our lives. We can be sure she will always hear our prayers because she was willing to help in our salvation. Her whole life on earth was spent in the accomplishment of this goal. It brought her many sorrows. Appealing to his mother with our prayers will mean much to Jesus in answering them. We do not worship Mary as a god but rather as the mother of Jesus, the Divine Son. When we pray to her it is always to ask her intercession with her Son.

Holy Mary, Mother of God, pray for us sinners now and at the hour of our death. Amen.

In this second part of the prayer we plead for Mary's intercession on our behalf before her all powerful and divine Son whom she held in her arms as a baby. We can always be sure she will help us in this regard because she was willing to help in our salvation. Mary spent her whole life on earth helping her son in the accomplishment of this goal. Therefore, you can see that appealing to this very special woman, His mother, will mean much to Him in answering our prayers.

The Hail Mary is the sweetest of all prayers between us, the children of God, and our mother, Mary, who was given to us by Christ while He was dying on His Cross. Mary so pleased God that He used His Divine power to take her body and soul into heaven when she died. He then proclaimed her **QUEEN OF HEAVEN**.

The truth of the Assumption of Mary into Heaven was declared Church Dogma in the Holy Year 1950 by Pope Pius XII.

AN ACT OF CONTRITION

The Act of Contrition is the one prayer that we should WANT to know desperately. Because we are so prone to sin we need this prayer on the tip of our tongue at all times. Contrition means sorrow. We cannot be considered confirmed Christians if we cannot feel true sorrow for our offenses to God. To consider this a prayer we MUST learn is to miss the whole spirit of the prayer itself.

Oh my God, I am heartily sorry for having offended thee.

These words are clear in their meaning but it is the FEEL-ING with which they are said that gives them their

VALUE. Though a priest in the confessional cannot KNOW this value, God can.

And I detest all my sins.

We must hate the times when we are offensive to God in order to be sorry and hope to change. Sin is an offense to our loving God through a violation of the laws He gave and enshrined in our hearts and conscience. It is true that a violation of these laws offends Him but it also kills the life of grace in our lives. In addition, it hurts others who are affected by our sin. You have heard that anyone can do as they please as long as it does not hurt anyone else. This is a lie. It is never true. All of our lives we are affecting others with our life and what we do with it.

Because I dread the loss of heaven and fear the pains of hell.

Jesus has told us that there is a hell where He does not dwell and we can never hope to see God face to face. Jesus has told us clearly that His kingdom is heaven; that the Father is in heaven. It is where we are promised we will go if we keep His commandments. He has also told us that there is a hell where He does not dwell and can never hope to be seen. Those who do not keep His commandments will go there. It is right and good that we should dread the loss of heaven and the pains of hell where we can never hope to see God face to face.

But most of all because they offend thee, my God, who are all good and deserving of all my love.

These words convey the real meaning of our sorrow for sin. Love of God should dominate our lives – not fear of him. But in order to have this frame of mind, we should be free from sin because sin has no part with God.

I firmly resolve, with the help of thy grace, to confess my sins, to do penance and to amend my life. Amen.

By our strength alone we are unable to overcome our inclination to sin. But with God's help, or grace, we can overcome every temptation to do evil. God has given us the means through which to accomplish this by confession of our sins to His representative on earth, our priest. He is the mediator for us, gives us advice on how to control our evil inclinations and sets an appropriate penance for us to do in reparation for our sins. By doing so he helps us to amend our lives. But it is our own intention to amend our life that must accompany His blessing.

This form of an Act of Contrition may be modified but not its meaning. The prayer should be said after the examination of your conscience and before entering the confessional. The examination of conscience should take into consideration – but not be limited to – the Ten Commandments of God, the six Precepts of the Catholic Church and the Two Great Commandments of Jesus. Sometimes the priest may ask you to say an Act of Contrition while in the confessional and you should be prepared to do so.

This prayer is always a powerful and appropriate prayer to say at night before going to sleep. It brings a peace to your sleep that nothing else can. If you make it a habit to say this prayer and really mean it, you can avoid many temptations to commit sin in your daily life.

THE NICENE CREED

The word "creed" means belief. According to the Catholic Encyclopedia, the Nicene Creed is the profession of the Christian Faith common to the Catholic Church, to all the Eastern Churches separated from Rome, and to most of the Protestant denominations. The Catholic Encyclopedia states that "Various hypotheses are offered to account for the tradition that the Niceno-Constantinopolitan symbol originated with the Council of Constantinople, but none of them is satisfactory. Whatever be its origin, the fact is that the council of Chalcedon (451) attributed it to the Council of Constantinople, and if it was not actually composed in that council, it was adopted and authorized by the Fathers assembled as a true expression of the Faith."

What we should be interested in is the long history of this beautiful salutation of praise to God of what we believe Him to be. The Apostles' Creed is a slightly shortened version of the Nicene Creed and is used sometimes at a Mass for children. The Nicene Creed is said at Masses all over the world every day. It contains *all* of the beliefs *essential* for us to believe in order to be members of the Catholic Church. This creed should be memorized in our hearts so that we never forget it.

WE BELIEVE IN ONE GOD, THE FATHER THE ALMIGHTY, MAKER OF HEAVEN AND EARTH, OF ALL THAT IS SEEN AND UNSEEN.

By this statement we tell God we believe in Him as the Creator of this world and all those things which we do see and even those we cannot see or totally understand with our finite mind.

WE BELIEVE IN ONE LORD, JESUS CHRIST, THE ONLY SON OF GOD, ETERNALLY BEGOTTEN OF THE FATHER, GOD FROM GOD, LIGHT FROM LIGHT, TRUE GOD FROM TRUE GOD, BEGOTTEN NOT MADE, ONE IN BEING WITH THE FATHER. THROUGH HIM ALL THINGS WERE MADE.

By saying this we acknowledge that Jesus Christ is one with the Father; that He is the Second Person of the Trinity, but that He always existed from the beginning of time. We believe that He is the Creator of all things.

FOR US MEN AND FOR OUR SALVATION HE CAME DOWN FROM HEAVEN, BY THE POWER OF THE HOLY SPIRIT HE WAS BORN OF THE VIRGIN MARY, AND BECAME MAN.

We acknowledge our belief that Jesus is the promised Messiah of the Old Testament; that through the power of the Holy Spirit, the virgin girl, Mary, conceived Him in her womb; that Jesus Christ is both God and man.

FOR OUR SAKE HE WAS CRUCIFIED UNDER PONTIUS PILATE: HE SUFFERED, DIED AND WAS BURIED. ON THE THIRD DAY HE ROSE AGAIN IN FULFILLMENT OF THE SCRIPTURES; HE ASCENDED INTO HEAVEN AND IS SEATED AT THE RIGHT HAND OF THE FATHER.

Christ's purpose was accomplished through his death on the cross. Our salvation means victory over death and we are promised life eternal when we die in His grace. His resurrection is proof that this is true. He is waiting for us in heaven where he sits at the right hand of the Father.

HE WILL COME AGAIN IN GLORY TO JUDGE THE LIVING AND THE DEAD AND HIS KINGDOM WILL HAVE NO END.

Christ will come again to claim us, body and soul. We are promised a place in heaven where we will live with Him in His kingdom forever.

WE BELIEVE IN THE HOLY SPIRIT, THE LORD, THE GIVER OF LIFE, WHO PROCEEDS FROM THE FATHER AND THE SON. WITH THE FATHER AND THE SON HE IS WORSHIPPED AND GLORIFIED. HE HAS SPOKEN THROUGH THE PROPHETS.

Here we affirm our belief in the Third Person of the Trinity and acknowledge that The Holy Spirit has spoken to us through the prophets of the Old Testament. The Holy Spirit still speaks to us today through the Pope and the Holy men and women of the Church. We especially acknowledge that the Holy Spirit has spoken to us through Mary, the mother of Jesus. She has made many appearances on earth since she was assumed into heaven, body and soul.

WE BELIEVE IN ONE HOLY, CATHOLIC AND APOSTOLIC CHURCH. WE ACKNOWLEDGE ONE BAPTISM FOR THE FORGIVENESS OF SINS. WE LOOK FOR THE RESURRECTION OF THE DEAD, AND THE LIFE OF THE WORLD TO COME. AMEN.

We acknowledge our belief in the Catholic Church founded by Christ and nourished by the teaching of the apostles, the Pope, the cardinals, the bishops and priests and also us, the laity.

We also acknowledge the necessity of baptism which Christ told us we must have in order to allow us the hope of heaven since we are born after our first parents caused this hope to be denied us by original sin.

We agree that we must be forgiven our personal sins since that is how we keep this hope alive all our lives.

We have the promise of heaven and life eternal with God. With this promise we are able to live our lives with this thought uppermost in our minds.

The strength of our faith in this creed will determine the manner in which we live our lives as Catholic Christians. We must believe and practice all of these truths to be truly Catholic. The words of this Creed make our presence at the celebration of the Mass important to God for it is our expression to Him of our belief in Him and our love for Him. It is important to show in a public way that we believe the truths He has revealed through His Son, Jesus

Christ and the Holy Spirit who moves through this world at all times. The Mass with this Creed is our most important statement that we are Christians and Catholic. It brings forth our final exclamation of formal prayer in which we recognize the Trinity of God as always existing. This prayer reaffirms our belief in the Trinity when we make the Sign of the Cross and it explains infinity.

GLORY BE TO THE FATHER

AND TO THE SON,

AND TO THE HOLY SPIRIT:
AS IT WAS IN THE BEGINNING,

IS NOW,

AND EVER SHALL BE,

WORLD WITHOUT END.

AMEN.

These are the prayers that all who want to participate in Catholic life must know. There are others, of course, very special ones that you will want to learn and use daily. The Rosary is one such prayer. This beautiful prayer takes you through the life of Christ and has been especially given to us by His mother, Mary, for the benefit of keeping us close to the life of her Divine Son. Acts of Love, Hope, Humility, etc., are especially recommended for morning and night prayers.

Most important though are the times when we speak to God from our hearts in our own way. He created us each to be unique and it is through our own personal prayer and meditation with Him that He is able to enjoy the uniqueness that He put into each one of us. Jesus taught His apostles to pray through His example. He went away by himself and spent many hours in meditation and prayer with His heavenly Father.

Through these private times of prayer you will learn the difference between prayer and meditation. It has been said that prayer is the time we spend talking with God. Meditation, however, is the time we allow God the necessary silence to talk with us. This happens only when we are willing to spend time with God alone everyday of our lives. It is an experience that no one can tell you about. You must come to know it alone—with God. There will be no other experience like it in your life.

The Ten Commandments

People of every nation, in every age, the world over, have tried to set up rules and regulations for the orderly living of communities. Great volumes of books have been written to contain these rules or laws. Some men and women throughout history have become famous for their ability to proclaim laws in such a way that they profoundly affected their fellow man, sometimes for good, sometimes for evil.

One such man who is responsible for mankind receiving the most famous set of laws did not write them himself and did not want to become a servant of the Master who gave them to him. But he will always be remembered as one of the most significant persons in the political and religious history of the world. The principal reason for this remembrance is the set of laws he brought to mankind from God.

The great life of Moses is recorded in the Old Testament Book of Exodus. It is a glorious one of accomplishments he realized and the manner in which God revealed Himself to mankind through Moses. The tragedies and difficulties of this unique man, who came to intimately know and love God as perhaps no other human being has, are an example to us of how God can take our lives and make something superlative of them.

When God summoned Moses to the mountain to speak with Him, Moses was bewildered about the things that God was asking him to do. He was reluctant to believe that he could do them. He was able to accomplish the tasks God set before him only by his faith in God. We must remember that Moses was born at a time in the history of mankind when it was very dangerous to believe in the One True God. God chose Moses to prove to mankind that He really LIVES and has POWER. His power over the natural order of the universe was demonstrated time and time again through Moses. He did this to prove a religious truth for the benefit of men of all times that we might believe in HIM and FOLLOW HIM.

Jesus spoke about this in the parable of the rich man and Lazarus:

Once there was a rich man who dressed in purple and linen and feasted splendidly every day. At his gate lay a beggar named Lazarus who was covered with sores. Lazarus longed to eat the scraps that fell from the rich man's table. The dogs even came and licked his sores. Eventually the beggar died. He was carried by angels to the bosom of Abraham. The rich man likewise died and was buried. From the abode of the dead where he was in torment, he raised his eyes and saw Abraham afar off, and Lazarus resting in his bosom.
He called out, 'Father Abraham, have pity on me. Send Lazarus to dip the tip of his finger in water to refresh my tongue, for I am tortured in these flames.' 'My child,' replied Abraham, 'remember that you were well off in your lifetime, while Lazarus was in misery. Now he has found consolation here, but you have found torment. And that is not all. Between you and us there is fixed a great abyss, so that those who might wish to cross from here to you cannot do so, nor can anyone cross from your side to us.'
'Father, I ask you then,' the rich man said, 'send him to my father's house where I have five brothers. Let him be a warning to them so that they may not end in this place of torment.' Abraham answered, 'They have Moses and the prophets. Let them hear them.' 'No, Father Abraham,' replied the rich man. 'But if someone would only go to them from the dead, then they would repent.' Abraham said to him, 'If they do not listen

to Moses and the prophets, they will not be convinced even if one should rise from the dead.'

Luke 16:19-31

God has given us Moses and the prophets to teach us concerning His truths and His laws. To ignore these men is to court the disaster of the rich man. We ignore these at the risk of eternal life. That is quite a risk to take. God has put into the natural order of the world from the time of its creation certain laws affecting mankind. These were not spoken but were observable in nature and always there. God chose the time, the place and the man who would receive these laws from Him. Now they would be spoken to mankind. These laws are embodied in the Ten Commandments that God wrote on stone tablets for Moses to give to His people. They made clear statements of God's will for mankind to live in peace and harmony all the days of his life on earth. They were made to put an end to the confusion of the people about God and His creation and how He expected His people to live.

Then the LORD said to Moses, 'Write down these words, for in accordance with them I have made a covenant with you and with Israel.' So Moses stayed there with the LORD for forty days and forty nights, without eating any food or drinking any water, and he wrote on the tablets the words of the covenant, the ten commandments.

Exodus 34:27,28

When the LORD had finished speaking to Moses on Mount Sinai, he gave him the two tablets of the commandments, the stone tablets inscribed by God's own finger.

Exodus 31:18

The "shall nots" in these Commandments are a road map for the happiness of mankind. They are a great gift from God to us, His people.

The Ten Commandments present each of us with the same test that God gave to our first parents. He told them NOT to eat the fruit from a certain tree or they would die. In these Commandments God tells us NOT to do certain things or we will die. If we disobey, as did our first parents, our souls will be so seriously injured that they cannot live with the grace of His life in them. Just as the tempter came to Adam and Eve in the Garden of Eden, so he comes to us, too, and assures us that these "shall nots" are simply designed to deny us the pleasures of life. The tempter assures us that it will not hurt us to disobey them. The devil lies.

Just as Adam and Eve were dismissed from their paradise of life with God, so, too, we will be dismissed from our life of grace with God if we say, "I will not obey." In God's merciful love He has left us a ray of hope while we are on earth that we can always be reunited with Him and again partake of his grace. GOD WILL NEVER TOTALLY ABANDON US. THERE IS ALWAYS A WAY TO RETURN TO HIM AS LONG AS WE LIVE.

The Ten Commandments should be memorized. They have endured through many generations of people. Billions of people have relied on them for truth in living a good life and have verified the truth of these laws. These people are a witness to you from generation to generation that these laws are true and work for good in your life when you obey them.

You have to decide whether or not you will accept the restrictions these laws place on the way you live your life. No one can do this for you. In order to do this in a conscientious way you must consider what these laws will allow you to do with your life and what they will not allow you to do. Always remember that these laws were given to you out of LOVE. They are not designed to DENY you anything that is good for you. Rather, they show you how to ATTAIN happiness in your own life.

Suppose you decide not to obey these laws of God. Does that mean that they are not true and in force? No, it does not. These laws are true whether you decide to obey them or not. And you will suffer the consequences that flow from disobedience to them whether you want to or not. These laws are the authority outside yourself that you should obey. Let's talk about them specifically:

I

I, the LORD, am your God, who brought you out of the land of Egypt, that place of slavery. You shall not have other gods besides me. You shall not carve idols for yourselves in the shape of anything in the sky above or on the earth below or in the waters beneath the earth; you shall not bow down before them or worship them. For I, the LORD, your God, am a jealous God, inflicting punishment for their fathers' wickedness on the children of those who hate me, down to the third and fourth generation; but bestowing mercy own to the thousandth generation, on the children of those who love me and keep my commandments.

Exodus 20:2-6

It is in the very nature of each person to want to do something great with his or her life. In other words, we want to consecrate ourselves to some great goal. But we are mortals, living in a world not of our creation; we are only a part of its creation. Because we are such mortals, we will always yearn to worship that which is greater than we are – our Creator.

We have been given the power to reason – uniquely. No other part of creation has this power. So, it is possible for us to come to the conclusion that our Creator lives and that we should love and adore Him for the mighty and wonderful things He has done for us. But not everyone will use the ability to reason in this way.

There is also another power loose in the world in which we live; the power of evil. Its purpose is to prevent us from paying homage and tribute to that which is good and true. This power is exerted in the world in subtle ways—in the form of strange gods; e.g., power, lust, money, fame, etc. Each generation of people, every individual in it, must constantly cope with these two forces in their lives. It is the cause of much confusion for these two powers often cloak themselves in disguises that are not easily recognizable as GOOD and EVIL.

That which is good may often come into our lives in the form of hardship, trial and grief and we are tempted to trust our FEELINGS that this cannot be good. On the other hand, that which is evil is often cloaked in many disguises such as pleasure, curiosity, self-enlightenment, etc. These please our senses and make us FEEL very good. Therefore, we are tempted to think it cannot be evil.

If we cannot trust ourselves, our feelings, then whom or what can we trust? Our fellow man? He is subject to the same mortal limitations that we have. If we are to have any guide through this life whom we can trust, it must be He who created us and still cares for us. He told us: "I am the Lord Thy God." We cannot worship strange gods that appear in our lives and they are always there in every generation.

Call to mind the scene at the foot of the mountain when Moses came down and saw the people who had witnessed the mighty power of God when He led them out of the land of Egypt as slaves, worshiping a golden calf! In just a short time (approximately six weeks) after God had delivered them from slavery through His power to suspend the natural order before their very eyes, they had grown weary of worshiping a God they could not see and who made demands on them. So, they made a god they could see and were deceived into believing it was real. Because of their disobedience to Him, God let them wander in the desert for forty years when they could have reached the Promised Land in only about three more weeks.

It is never different in any generation. We have witnesses to the power of God in every age and we are witnesses to His power every day and yet the power of evil confuses our minds and makes us subject to its influence. Our only hope is to acknowledge God for who He is and constantly ask His help in keeping the strange gods who come into our lives from dominating them and ruining them. The way that we do this is by consecrating ourselves to the ONE TRUE GOD and making heaven with Him our goal.

II

You shall not take the name of the LORD, your God, in vain. For the LORD will not leave unpunished him who takes his name in vain.

Exodus 20:7

The word "vain" means to have no value, be worthless, empty, without force or effect, to be futile and fruitless. If you recognize the REALITY OF GOD and the fact that HE LIVES and is all-powerful and can do anything, do you also begin to see the love with which He gave us this commandment?

When you believe in the reality of God, then you know He can do anything. This knowledge should produce an awesome respect in us. But we must also begin to realize the power we have as the children of God in being able to approach Him and ask personal favors of Him knowing full well that HE has the POWER to grant them if they are good for us.

The power of God is not empty nor is it fruitless. It does have force and effect and it has real value and real significance. It *is the greatest power there is.* To call on it and not really believe in it is insulting to God. Can you begin to see why this is one of the greatest laws of all time? Why it is so important for us to know and believe in it?

It is the one law that calls forth the power of God through His name. Do not use it in vain or your relationship with God will be seriously hurt. For instance, would you go to your mortal father and ask him for favors that you do not believe he will give you? Don't you think you might be a little neurotic to perform such a useless gesture? And what if he sees through your motives? Won't he be deeply hurt that you treated his love for you with so much shallowness?

God is our Father too. And we are His children. We must be very careful how we treat His love for us if we do not wish to hurt Him deeply.

III

Remember to keep holy the sabbath day. Six days you may labor and do all your work, but the seventh day is the sabbath of the LORD, your God. No work may be done then either by you, or your son or daughter, or your male or female slave, or your beast, or by the alien who lives with you. In six days the LORD made the heavens and the earth, the sea and all that is in them; but on the seventh day he rested. That is why the LORD has blessed the sabbath day and made it holy.

Exodus 20:9-11

"To rest with God" is the true meaning of this command-ment. Our most precious gift is life. Next to that is time in which to live life. God, who created us, also created the order in which our lives would be spent in terms of seg-ments of time. Since God created our bodies, He knew that they required rest in every twenty-four hour period. Have you ever wondered why everyone in the world lies down at night to rest? He created our spirits too and they need time to rekindle and refresh at least once in every seven-day period of time. Without nightly rest and spiri-tual refreshment, we suffer a loss of bodily and spiritual health. We become sick people without both kinds of rest.

It is for this reason that God admonishes us to remember to keep the Sabbath holy by resting our bodies from hard work and our minds from mental toil. We need to get away from the daily routine of our lives every seventh day and to keep that day holy by living it in recreation with God and His creation.

In all of its centuries of existence, the Church that Jesus established has made only six laws binding on its mem-bers. One of these precepts concerns the manner in which we spend time to rest with God. This Church law tells us to gather with other members of our faith and cel-ebrate the Mass. We do this so that we can really and actually meet with God and He can really and actually meet with us. He comes to us in the Holy Eucharist and His altar is the only place on earth where this happens. No matter what other ways we honor God on this seventh day, none is more important than meeting with Him at Mass and receiving Him in the Holy Eucharist. It is our direct encounter with God.

For many Catholics this is the only time during the week when this direct meeting with God takes place. We need His Eucharistic sustenance to sustain us the other six days of the week. It is easy to become sick in spirit without this spiritual food.

How we spend the rest of this seventh day will determine our own unique way of telling God how much we appreciate Him as Creator of all living things. Mothers and fathers love to see their children happily playing together and enjoying the benefits of the home they have provided, within the rules of orderly living. Our heavenly Father is no different. God's creation is our home on earth and He enjoys watching us enjoy the world He created for us and doing all of the recreational things we like doing.

If we selfishly take advantage of this day set aside for worship of God and rest for our bodies and spirits by failing to worship Him on this day, then we risk His wrath. If we seek our own gratification, without God in the picture, then we seriously offend Him who made this day possible.

IV

Honor your father and your mother, that you may have a long life in the land which the LORD, your God, is giving you.

Exodus 20:12

This is the first of the Commandments telling us how to conduct our lives on earth with regard to each other. It is fitting that it should be first because our parents are those people whose loving act made our lives possible.

Honor means to give great respect or hold in high regard. But think about who it is that receives the most from obedience to this commandment? Is it the parents? Think about it again. If you always conduct your life in such a way that no shame or disgrace comes to your parents because of your actions, who benefits the most? You do, of course. It means that in your own life you are doing only those things that bring honor to you, and thereby to your mother and father.

It also means that the parents who gave you life and nourished you through your young life will never know shame on your account. It is the one thing all parents want for their child and for themselves.

And what determines honor or shame in a person's life? It is in the keeping or breaking of these Commandments of God. Only the wisdom of God could give us this simple commandment whereby we show love to someone else (our parents), and receive a direct blessing in our lives by the rewards we receive for the way we live.

V

You shall not kill.

Exodus 20:13

This Commandment reminds us that God is the giver of life and we are not to take away His right to determine when any person's life is over. This is the province of God alone.

When someone breaks this Commandment by killing one of our fellow men, he forces us to take action as a community of people because we are now all in danger of our lives. With this Commandment we are answerable to God as a community of people rather than as individuals. When someone commits murder we cannot avoid making a judgment about whether this killing was done under circumstances not likely to happen again or whether that person will kill again if not deterred.

How to make this judgment is a question that has plagued mankind from the very beginning of time. In the Old Testament Moses interpreted this commandment for the people in a manner which meant that if you took another person's life from him then you must realize that your fellow citizens would require that you give your life for the one that you took. When Cain slew Abel he was so fearful of his fellow man killing him that God put a mark on him to protect him from this kind of death. God did not require the life of Cain for the murder of Abel. Rather, He protected a murderer.

In the New Testament, Jesus added a new commandment—*Love one another as I have loved you.* This causes us to wonder if Moses' interpretation was too harsh because Christ gave up His life for us and did not require ours in return. In St. John's Gospel, Chapter 8:3-11 there is a discourse about capital punishment.

> The scribes and Pharisees led a woman forward who had been caught in adultery. They made her stand there in front of everyone. 'Teacher,' they said to him, 'this woman has been caught in the act of adultery. In the law, Moses ordered such women to be stoned. What do you have to say about the case?' (They were posing this question to trap him, so that they could have something to accuse him of.) Jesus bent down and started tracing on the ground with his finger. When they persisted in their questioning, he straightened up and said to them, 'Let the man among you who has no sin be the first to cast a stone at her.' A second time he bent down and wrote on the ground. Then the audience drifted away one by one beginning with the elders. This left him alone with the woman, who continued to stand there before him. Jesus finally straightened up and said to her, 'Woman, where did they all disappear to? Has no one condemned you?' 'No one, sir,' she answered. Jesus said, 'Nor do I condemn you. You may go. But from now on, avoid this sin.'
>
> John 8:3-11

Jesus seems to be teaching us in this parable that it is wrong to take the life of another because he has committed a sin against His Commandments. Perhaps God wants all of us to always have the opportunity to change our lives because He will forgive our sin if we are truly sorry for it and repent of having done it.

Yet we are charged with a duty if we intend to live as a community of peaceful people. The murderer must be deterred from committing this sin again. We seem to be charged with the obligation of finding a way to deter people from killing without taking their life in return for the murder they committed. Banishment from society by being placed in a prison away from the community has been the answer. It is not a perfect answer but it does allow the person the opportunity God wants him to have to repent of his grave sin.

In the United States of America it is possible, by law, to kill a conceived child in the womb without being punished for it by the government. Christians will always be held to a higher standard than governmental law. It is a mortal sin to kill in this way according to God's law. There will be times when we are required to live above governmental law when civil law conflicts with the law of God.

The Commandment against killing has more meaning and application than just the taking of another's life. It is possible to kill a person's good name by gossip and rumor. Even if the rumor is true it is wrong to repeat it unnecessarily. A person may sin against this Commandment by doing things to his body that will eventually kill it. For example, drinking alcohol to excess over a long period of time, using harmful drugs that your body does not need for its well being, using violence toward another person or unjustified anger over such a period of time that it will kill their spirit.

If all people obey this Commandment, and the others that deal with how we are to live as a community, order and peace are brought into our lives. By disobeying the Commandments, order and peace are shattered with chaos, and fear takes its place. As a community of people it becomes difficult to know and agree on how to deal with such disobedience. It brings complex problems into our lives that were not meant to be there. We are only capable of dealing with them in our imperfect, human way. Our only hope is that God is merciful and will forgive us, as a people, if we commit sin while trying to handle the sins of others.

VI

You shall not commit adultery.

Exodus 20:14

The meaning of the words "to adulterate" is to make something inferior, impure or not genuine, as by adding a poor or improper substance. By giving us this commandment God is telling us that He does not want us to adulterate the loving act of sexual union between a husband and wife by partaking of this privilege with another person not a husband or wife.

Sexual union is the means by which God has given to mankind the POWER to create new life on earth, generation after generation. It is also the complete way in which husband and wife express their total love and commitment to each other. God made a woman for man when He said:

"It is not good for the man to be alone. I will make a suitable partner for him."

Genesis 2:18

Further on He said:

> "That is why a man leaves his father and mother and clings to his wife, and the two of them become one body."
>
> *Genesis 2:24*

These words spoken by God tell us clearly that one man is to take one wife and that they are to live together as husband and wife and have sexual union with no one else. To use the loving act of sexual union in any other way is to adulterate it, make it inferior, impure, not genuine.

It is also the way in which children are to be nourished by a loving mother and father. When adultery is introduced into the life of the family, it brings sorrow and sadness that infect the entire community in which they live. It may bring such emotional grief to the marriage partner that love may die. Divorce may be the solution the couple use to lessen the intensity of their pain. But this solution brings chaos into the lives of the children of this family and the community in which they live.

Further, we are in danger of contracting serious venereal diseases that might destroy our own life. But, even more important than these is the fact that it causes mortal sin to infect our spirit or soul. This can deny us the right to heaven if we persist in violating this Commandment without repenting for our sin.

God is telling us that only a husband and wife may partake of sexual union. Any man who takes another woman, other than his wife, in this way, or any woman who takes another man, other than her husband, in this way, is an adulterer and will suffer the consequences that come with committing this sin.

God is also telling us that sexual union is only for a man and a woman who have made a serious commitment to love each other as husband and wife. This sexual act is for sacramental marriage only. It is called fornication when sexual union is used in this improper way. Without this sacramental commitment to love as husband and wife, sexual union is strictly forbidden to us as a means of attaining happiness on earth and heaven afterward.

VII

You shall not steal.

Exodus 20:15

To steal means to take that which belongs to another. By this Commandment God gives us the right to have and own things of our very own. This Commandment should be the basis for human rights all over the world and no government should take it away from us. There are many ways in which we may steal from another person.

As human beings we have a right to be paid a just wage for work that we do but we have an obligation to our employer to give him just time and labor for the wages he pays us. We have a right to be charged a just price for items we buy but we have an obligation to pay for these purchases and not to cheat the seller out of his just compensation. We have a right to purchase items that are for sale but we are forbidden to take those items by stealing them. We have a right to use property which we call "public" or for general use by everyone but we have a duty to care for it – not to damage or spoil it as a result of our using it. This Commandment also binds us to make restitution or pay damages to those whom we injure. It forbids our keeping that which we have obtained by stealing.

This Commandment is an absolute necessity to the orderly living that should go on in community life. When it is broken not only God is injured, but other members of the community as well. Punishment is necessary in order to preserve orderly living. The punishment must be just according to the seriousness of the offense. We must always remember that God will take care of eternal punishment but men must administer earthly punishment in order that the community of man will not suffer endlessly the hardships created by those who will not follow this law.

VIII

You shall not bear false witness against your neighbor.

Exodus 20:16

No man lives alone on this earth. We all have to trust one another's word in all of our dealings with each other. There is probably no hurt more deeply felt than to have our friends and associates say or tell untrue things about us in a deliberate way. There are times that such an untruth can be very damaging to us in a financial way or by ruining our reputation.

Yet, even greater harm is done to the person who tells an untruth for the conscience of that person will forever bother him until he is relieved of his guilt and makes restitution. Our conscience is for the purpose of telling us what is good and what is evil. The proof of conscience is told in this saying:

"The wicked man flees although no one pursues him; but the just man, like a lion, feels sure of himself."

Proverbs 28:1

Conscience is that force which is pursuing us when we have done wrong to our neighbor. When we break this Commandment, the orderliness of the community is disturbed for those sitting in judgment are denied that which they must have for the pursuit of justice – truth. Yet it is not an easy Commandment to keep. Telling the truth when to do so will not mean any particular hurt to us is easy, but what is ALWAYS difficult is to tell the truth when we know it will hurt US.

IX

You shall not covet your neighbor's house.

Exodus 20:17

X

You shall not covet your neighbor's wife,
nor his male or female slave, nor his ox or ass,
nor anything else that belongs to him.

Exodus 20:17

To covet means to crave or long for some person or some thing that we have no right to and which does not belong to us. Are these two Commandments really necessary since the Sixth Commandment already forbids us from committing adultery and the Seventh Commandment forbids us from stealing? They are because these two Commandments against coveting forbid our even LONG-ING FOR or WANTING that which belongs to another person. The ninth Commandment warns us that if in our hearts we long and crave for that which belongs to another person we shall soon be trying to possess it by our actions. The tenth commandment warns us that if we covet another person's husband or wife in our hearts, we shall soon be trying to possess him or her by our deeds or actions.

If we want and yearn for that which can never rightfully belong to us, there will be no end to the deceits and lies we engage in with our attempts to obtain the unobtainable. Eventually we will commit a grave sin. We are expressly forbidden to even yearn for another man's wife or another woman's husband or their goods.

God is telling us not to envy what others have but rather to go out and seek our own special person to love in a marital way. He wants us to work and obtain our own wealth without wasting our time wanting what we do not have a right to and which can never justly belong to us.

A person seeking confirmation in the Catholic Church is not too young to understand these Commandments and to see the peace and order that prevail when any group of people use them as a basis for community living. Even when some members of the community do not obey them, those who do gain a peace in their personal lives that is beautiful.

These Commandments give us rights which no person or government can justly take away from us because they contain our inheritance from God and are truly what make us "equal" with one another. Sometimes, however, governments pass laws that are in conflict with these Commandments. When this occurs, we must learn to live above the civil law and follow the law of God.

The Sacraments

The Real Presence of our loving Father is always with us on earth and this was never more true than when He sent His Son to us in the form of a man. Jesus lived here for thirty-three years. He taught by His example, His truth, and His Word. God remains with His people though Christ has ascended into heaven. While Christ was on earth He established His Church and the Seven Sacraments that we are about to discuss. These sacraments are the means by which God remains with His people at all times.

God promised that He would not leave us orphans, without the care of a Father. These sacraments are the means by which He keeps this promise to us. They are our umbilical cord with heaven because a sacrament is A HOLY ACT IN WHICH WE MEET GOD AND IN WHICH HE COMES TO MEET US. **All of them were given to us by Christ and can never be taken away by men.**

The traditions and ceremonies by which we receive these sacraments may change from time to time in accordance with the customs of the People of God through His Church. But, their substance NEVER changes. The sacraments are the SIGNS by which you recognize and know Christ's lovely bride – His Church. For her He died, so that she might live. We are the recipients of this most beautiful, unspeakable act of love.

BAPTISM

What is so important about our being baptized? What great harm will come to us if we are not? Will the symbolism of washing with water really cleanse something about us if done in the name of Christ?

We are certainly able to see with our own eyes that water is a great cleanser. Nothing in nature will wash away so much dirt as water. But what happens when it is used with the name of Christ in the sacrament of Baptism? To answer these questions, we have to look to Christ because He is the one who has told us to do this.

In the Third Chapter of the Book of John in the New Testament, Nicodemus, a Pharisee, came to Christ in the night because he was afraid to be seen with Him in the daytime. Nicodemus expresses our own bewilderment at this ritual of baptism. He senses that Christ must have come from God. He said to Christ:

> 'How can a man be born again once he is old?' retorted Nicodemus. 'Can he return to his mother's womb and be born over again?' Jesus replied:
>
> 'I solemnly assure you,
> no one can enter into God's kingdom
> without being begotten of water and Spirit.
> Flesh begets flesh,
> Spirit begets spirit.
> Do not be surprised that I tell you
> you must all be begotten from above.
> The wind blows where it will.
> You hear the sound it makes
> but you do not know where it comes from,
> or where it goes.
> So it is with everyone begotten of the Spirit.'

'How can such a thing happen?' asked Nicodemus. Jesus
responded: 'You hold the office of teacher of Israel and still
you do not understand these matters?

'I solemnly assure you,
we are talking about what we know,
we are testifying to what we have seen,
but you do not accept our testimony.

If you do not believe
when I tell you about earthly things,
how are you to believe
when I tell you about those of heaven?
No one has gone up to heaven
except the One who came down from there—
the Son of Man [who is in heaven].
Just as Moses lifted up the serpent in the desert,
so must the Son of Man be lifted up,
that all who believe
may have eternal life in him.

Yes, God so loved the world
that he gave his only Son,
that whoever believes in him may not die
but may have eternal life.
God did not send the Son into the world
to condemn the world
but that the world might be saved through him.
Whoever believes in him avoids condemnation,
but whoever does not believe is already condemned
for not believing in the name of God's only Son.

The judgment of condemnation is this:
the light came into the world,
but men loved darkness rather than light
because their deeds were wicked.
Everyone who practices evil
hates the light;
he does not come near it

for fear his deeds will be exposed.
But he who acts in truth
comes into the light,
to make clear
that his deeds are done in God.'

John 3:4-21

We are often confused about baptism the way
Nicodemus was. But Christ is educating him to the fact
that baptism is a spiritual act, the effects of which we
cannot see anymore than we can see the wind. Being
human, we naturally think of that which we know and can
see, the flesh being born from the mother's womb. But
Christ tells us plainly that the birth He is talking about is
of the spirit – that which we cannot see. He makes it clear
that this rebirth we must have comes about through
water and the Spirit. He wants us to trust His Word that
He knows the Spirit which will come and remove a stain
from us that will otherwise prevent us from entering the
kingdom of God.

Through this rebirth we are given a new life that will allow
us to enter God's kingdom and there is no other way for
us to get there. Christ tells us that we do not have to fully
understand this anymore than we understand where the
wind comes from and where it goes. We are simply to
trust Him as a witness from God that it is true.

Christ did not only TELL us that we should be baptized,
He allowed himself to be baptized as an EXAMPLE to us.

Later Jesus, coming from Galilee, appeared before John at
the Jordan to be baptized by him. John tried to refuse him
with the protest:

'I should be baptized by you, yet you come to me!' Jesus
answered: 'Give in for now. We must do this if we would fulfill
all of God's demands.' So John gave in. After Jesus was baptized he came directly out of the water. Suddenly the sky

opened and he saw the Spirit of God descend like a dove and
hover over him. With that, a voice from the heavens said,
'This is my beloved Son. My favor rests on him.'

Matthew 3:13-17

Can you really imagine this scene happening in your
mind? Can you put yourself in the place of the people
who were there and wonder at what your reaction would
have been to this extraordinary event? Only when you
can, and you believe it did happen, are you really convinced of the truth that Christ really is the Son of God. A
voice from heaven saying that this is His Beloved Son in
whom He is well pleased cannot be ignored.

Once you know that this happened, you must accept or
reject Christ as the Son of God. Not just teacher, good
man, phenomenal human being – but Son of God!
Acceptance of this will change your life. You will want
what Christ is offering in baptism – entrance into the
kingdom of God.

Christ not only told us to be baptized and submitted
Himself to baptism as an example for us, He provided the
way and the means by which every generation can receive
this new life. After His resurrection, the eleven disciples
went into Galilee to the mountain where Jesus had directed them to go. The eleven disciples made their way to
Galilee, to the mountain to which Jesus had summoned
them. At the sight of Him, those who had entertained
doubts fell down in homage. Jesus came forward and
addressed them in these words:

'Full authority has been given to me
both in heaven and on earth;
go, therefore, and make disciples of all the nations.
Baptize them in the name
"of the Father,
and of the Son,
and of the Holy Spirit."

> Teach them to carry out everything I have commanded you.
> And know that I am with you always, until the end of the
> world!'
>
> Matthew 28:18-20

By this act and by these words Christ made our rebirth in
the Spirit possible. He tells us that He has been given the
power to do this and that He will remain with us for all
time. But more than this He makes it clear that He has
given full authority to His disciples to perform the sacrament of Baptism for us.

A **PRIEST** administers the Sacrament of Baptism in a
special ceremony in the Catholic Church. It is usually
administered to infants when they are very young, but
**BAPTISM CAN BE ADMINISTERED TO ANYONE AT
ANY TIME.**

Catholic parents want their children baptized when they
are infants. They want them to be members of the of the
Church and to be able to enter the kingdom of God as
Christ promised they would if they die before reaching an
age of reason sufficient to determine the renewal of this
baptism in the Sacrament of Confirmation. The child's
parents choose godparents who are practicing Catholics
so that their child will have someone to look after the
spiritual life of their child in the event that the parents
should die or for some other reason be unable to do so.
At the special baptismal ceremony, the godparents
answer for the child the questions the priest asks which
bring forth the Holy Spirit into the life of the child as the
priest pours water over the head of the child. The spiritual graces that baptism brings forth are life long in their
benefits.

**THE SACRAMENT OF BAPTISM IN THE CATHOLIC
CHURCH IS RECEIVED ONLY ONCE.**

In cases of emergency, anyone may baptize another person by pouring water over the head and saying: "**I bap-**

tize you in the name of the Father and of the Son and of the Holy Spirit. Amen." Such baptisms should be confirmed in the special church ceremony as soon as possible.

A conditional baptism may be administered to those who convert to the Catholic Church after they have already been baptized in another Christian faith.

This usually happens when there is some uncertainty about the validity of the convert's previous baptism. This might happen when the priest is unable to determine the true belief of the minister who presided over the original baptism.

There is another kind of baptism that takes into account those people who have never had the opportunity to hear the Word of God but who have lived their lives in harmony with the Ten Commandments and the natural law. This is called a **baptism of desire** and it comes to those people who have no knowledge of God except through their own sense and reason.

Even though Christ told the apostles to go to all nations baptizing in the name of the Father, the Son and the Holy Spirit, this has not yet been accomplished in the world. There are many people who have not yet been made aware of the teachings of Christ. If these people live their lives in accordance with the natural law, God will not deny them into the kingdom because they had no opportunity to reject His Son.

However, those who **KNOW OF CHRIST** and His teaching regarding Baptism will be making a serious error in their lives to ignore His Word of warning that only those who are born of water and the Spirit will enter the kingdom of God. Since this teaching profoundly affects our eternal life after we die, it is a very serious matter that all members of the Church will want to follow in their own lives and to pass on to their children as their most important heritage.

Parents are allowed the privilege of making this decision for their children until they reach an age of reason sufficient enough to decide for themselves about this matter. Making this decision requires much knowledge about Christ and His Church. This is the purpose of all religious instruction.

At your Confirmation you will be asked to renew your baptismal vows yourself. If you decide to renew these vows and receive the Sacrament of Confirmation, you join the Church in your own name, not that of your parents.

The benefits bestowed on persons who choose to be baptized are these:

> The person has the stain of original sin removed from the soul.

> The person becomes a child of God in the Spirit.

> The person becomes a member of the Catholic Church.

> The person gains a right to heaven.

> The person receives the grace of God in his or her life.

HOLY COMMUNION

The beliefs taught by the Catholic Church regarding the Sacrament of Holy Communion separate us doctrinally from many of our Christian brethren all over the world. It is not an easy sacrament in which to believe. Actually, it is probably the most difficult doctrine to accept in our faith.

To be a Catholic means to believe that the bread and wine on the altar are consecrated by the priest and changed into the **BODY AND BLOOD OF CHRIST** – actually. Now who wants to eat another's body and drink his blood? Why should we? It is repugnant to our very natures to do so. As with all the sacraments we must look to Christ for the answers to these mysterious questions because it is He who told us to do this.

Christ had chosen his apostles and they were following Him about as He preached. As He traveled, He taught them and performed miraculous cures throughout Judea. People could not help knowing that this man was very special – that He must have come from God —to be able to do these marvelous things and teach them in such a wonderful way the truths of life. They followed Him in droves over the hillsides and valleys wanting to hear more. But then, one day in Capernaum, after they had been with Him and listening to Him and partaking of the miracle of the loaves and fishes, He said to them:

'I assure you,
you are not looking for me because you have seen signs
but because you have eaten your fill of the loaves.

You should not be working for perishable food
but for food that remains unto life eternal,
food which the Son of Man will give you;
it is on him that God the Father has set his seal.'

At this they said to him, 'What must we do to perform the works of God?' Jesus replied:

'This is the work of God:
have faith in the One whom he sent.'

'So that we can put faith in you,' they asked him, 'what sign
are you going to perform for us to see? What is the "work"
you do? Our ancestors had manna to eat in the desert;
according to Scripture, "He gave them bread from the heavens to eat."' Jesus said to them:

'I solemnly assure you,
it was not Moses who gave you bread from the heavens;
it is my Father who gives you the real heavenly bread.
God's bread comes down from heaven
and gives life to the world.'
'Sir, give us this bread always,' they besought him.
Jesus explained to them:
I, myself am the bread of life.
No one who comes to me shall ever be hungry,
no one who believes in me shall ever thirst.
But as I told you –
though you have seen me, you still do not believe.
All that the Father gives me shall come to me;
no one who comes will I ever reject,
because it is not to do my own will
that I have come down from heaven,
but to do the will of him who sent me.

It is the will of him who sent me
that I should lose nothing of what he has given me;
rather, that I should raise it up on the last day.
Indeed, this is the will of my Father,
that everyone who looks upon the Son
and believes in him
shall have eternal life.
Him I will raise up on the last day.'

John 6: 26-40

Now the people were upset with Jesus because of what
He had said about being the bread of life and having
come down from heaven. These people knew his mother,

Mary, and Joseph, who they believed to be his father. They could not understand what He meant about coming down from heaven and they murmured about this among themselves. In answer, Jesus tells them:

'Stop your murmuring,' Jesus told them.
'No one can come to me
unless the Father who sent me draws him;
I will raise him up on the last day.
It is written in the prophets:
'They shall all be taught by God.'
Everyone who has heard the Father
and learned from him
comes to me.
Not that anyone has seen the Father –
only the one who is from God
has seen the Father.
Let me firmly assure you,
he who believes has eternal life.
'I am the bread of life.
Your ancestors ate manna in the desert, but they died.
This is the bread that comes down from heaven
for a man to eat and never die.
I myself am the living bread
come down from heaven.
If anyone eats this bread
he shall live forever;
the bread I will give
is my flesh, for the life of the world.'

John 6:43-51

With this explanation Jesus gave them (and us) the truth, straight out and without parable. Truth is often difficult to hear and hard to bear. These people who had been following Jesus were distraught over what He was saying to them. Many of them said:

'How can he give us his flesh to eat?'

John 6:52

Can you blame them? They could not understand how they were to make themselves do what He asked – eat his Body and drink his Blood. These words of Christ were, for those people at Capernaum, the same as they are for us today. We are bound under the same human limitations as they were. There is no answer to this but to trust Christ and know that He is Truth. Christ said to them as He says to us today:

'Let me solemnly assure you,
if you do not eat the flesh of the Son of Man
and drink his blood
you have no life in you.
He who feeds on my flesh
and drinks my blood
has life eternal,
and I will raise him up on the last day.
For my flesh is real food
and my blood real drink.
The man who feeds on my flesh
and drinks my blood
remains in me, and I in him.
Just as the Father who has life sent me
and I have life because of the Father,
so the man who feeds on me
will have life because of me.
This is the bread that came down from heaven.
Unlike your ancestors who ate and died nonetheless,
the man who feeds on this bread shall live forever.'
He said this in a synagogue instruction at Capernaum.

John 6:53-59

Now Christ makes it very clear that we MUST eat His Body and drink his Blood if we are to be brought to heaven and eternal life. It is important to know what Christ did at this point. He knew what these people were thinking. Many of them found this teaching too hard to hear and they left Him. Yet, He did not call them back and say to them that He really did not mean literally what He had said. Rather, He let the ones go who did not believe in Him and trust Him. Many of them could not give Him the kind of trust He was demanding. He asked his apostles:

'Do you want to leave me too?'

John 6:67

Simon Peter answered Him and his answer is the answer of every Catholic for centuries afterward:

'Lord, to whom shall we go? You have the words of eternal life. We have come to believe; we are convinced that you are God's holy one.'

John 6:68,69

Every Catholic must make the same choice as the people at Capernaum did that day long ago. Billions of people, generation after generation, century after century, have answered as Peter did. They have believed and relied on what Christ said at this historic place. Even now, all around the earth you can watch the lines of people who get up out of their pews when the Mass is being said. They line up to receive the bread the priest offers and hear what he says as he gives it to each one: **BODY OF CHRIST**.

But just as with all the sacraments, Christ does not leave us with His Word alone. He ate this bread himself as an example for us and left the way and means by which He continues to give us His life just as He promised He would.

At the time of the Last Supper, the apostles were gathered together with Christ for the Passover Feast. They were unaware of the important thing that was to take place at this special meal.

During the meal Jesus took bread, blessed it, broke it, and gave it to his disciples. 'Take this and eat it,' he said, 'this is my body.' Then he took a cup, gave thanks, and gave it to

them. 'All of you must drink from it,' he said, 'for this is my
blood, the blood of the covenant, to be poured out in behalf of
many for the forgiveness of sins.'

Matthew 26:26-28

Christ has now fulfilled His word at Capernaum and has
left us this most special of all sacraments, His very own
Body and Blood. It requires an act of faith on our part to
believe this but that is just what Christ wants and
demands of us just as He did the people at Capernaum.
If we do not believe, He will not stop us if we wish to go
away.

Many Christians the world over cannot bring themselves
to believe that Christ really meant what He said about
eating His Body and drinking His Blood and they interpret the words at the Last Supper to be only symbolic.
The Catholic Church is the principal religion of the world
that teaches He meant plainly what He said. The Holy
Eucharist is truly the Body and Blood of Christ. It is the
greatest treasure that Christ left for us on earth.

The Sacrament of Holy Communion is administered
DAILY in the Catholic Church. The power to consecrate
the bread and wine into the Body and Blood of Christ is
passed down through the centuries by bishops to priests.
The priest is the one who is ordained to make this sacrament possible to the people at the celebration of the
Mass. Without a priest the Mass cannot be said. In some
parishes the bread and wine, which has been previously
consecrated, may be given out by special persons trained
to do this called Extraordinary Ministers.

Because Catholics believe that the consecrated host is
really the Body and Blood of Christ our churches contain
tabernacles on the altars where the consecrated hosts
are kept in the sanctuary part of the church. Because
Christ is always there, a sanctuary lamp is kept burning at
all times. This is a distinguishing mark in all Catholic
churches.

In order to receive this sacrament we should follow the admonition of St. Paul in his letter to the Corinthians:

'This means that whoever eats the bread or drinks the cup of the Lord unworthily sins against the body and blood of the Lord. A man should examine himself first; only then should he eat of the bread and drink of the cup.'

1 Corinthians 11:27,28

The **REAL PRESENCE** of Christ in our Church means that we should be very careful of our behavior while in His Church. Christ is not just another person like us. He is our King and we should always come into His Presence in His Church with this in mind. This is His house.

Belief in the Real Presence is why we walk quietly in Church, never running. It is why we genuflect before entering the pew to sit down. We are acknowledging the presence of our King. For the same reason we genuflect whenever we are in front of God at the sanctuary entrance. If we come to Church when the Holy Eucharist is in Exposition, we genuflect on both knees to acknowledge that He has come out of the tabernacle in order for us to adore Him.

The language of God is silence. This is why we should remain quiet in Church unless we are praying publicly or singing our praises to our King as a community group.

God loves all virtue and modesty is certainly one that He wants from His children. For this reason we should go to His house dressed in a modest way at all times. On the occasions when Mass is celebrated, we should wear our better clothing as a sign of respect for Him. This is also a sign of respect that we have for ourselves and other members of the Church.

The time for showing special reverence for Christ is at the reception of His Body and Blood at Communion. We do this by approaching the altar in a slow, reverent manner with our hands folded in prayer. In some churches we still kneel at the altar rail while in others it has been removed and we stand to receive Him. This is the most awesome gift that anyone can ever receive. It is the food that sustains us in our efforts to lead a moral life from day to day or week to week.

Whether we stand or kneel, our attitude about His coming to us is what is important. We should approach the priest in a respectful manner with our hands folded until we are in front of him. If we intend to receive Christ by having the host placed on our tongue, we should hold our head well back and open our mouth wide enough for the priest to easily place the host on our tongue. The tongue should be protruded enough to easily receive the host.

If we intend to receive Christ by having the host placed in our hand, we put our cupped hands together in a position high enough for the priest to tell that we want to receive that way. The hand in which we wish to have the priest place the host should be in the upper position. The other hand should be directly under it so that when the host is placed in the upper hand, it can be retrieved quickly and placed in the mouth. This should be done while still facing the altar and taking a moment to make the Sign of the Cross. When we receive Communion in the hand we should never turn our back on the altar before placing the host in our mouth.

The form by which we receive Christ (by hand or by tongue) is not nearly so important as the fact that He is coming to us. His promise to always be with us is fulfilled. As we receive Communion it is important to remember what He said:

I am the bread of life.

John 6:48

The Catholic Church requires you to believe that the Holy Eucharist is all of the following:

That it is bread and wine changed into the Body and Blood of Christ;

That it is the reception of Jesus under the appearance of bread and wine;

That it is the Mass that is both a sacrifice and a meal;

That it is the replacement of the "bloody" sacrifice in the Old Testament that was accomplished by Jesus dying on the cross on Good Friday.

TWO requirements are made of you by the Catholic Church in order for you to receive Jesus in this manner. They are that:

You have no mortal sin in your life that you have not confessed. (This includes a lifestyle of presumed mortal sin, e.g., a confirmed Catholic living in a marriage situation not blessed by the Church or a divorced re-married Catholic.)

You observe the Eucharistic fast. (At present this means refraining from food and/or liquids, except water for ONE HOUR before you receive Holy Communion.

CONFESSION OF SINS
OR PENANCE

Many people do not see the necessity for private confession of sins. "Why should I?" they ask. "I can talk to God directly without the need of a priest to mediate for me." Some critics of confession go further and lament about the number of "hypocrites" who go to confession on Saturday and commit the same sins the rest of the week.

We must ask ourselves these questions, too. But, as with all the sacraments, we must go to Christ for the answers.

Christ went throughout Judea teaching and healing. Always, as He healed, He stressed the importance of the person's faith in the use of His healing power over their sickness. After He healed them, He told them to go and SIN NO MORE. Over and over He stressed the fact that SIN was like being SICK. It is like being unable to walk, to talk or to see.

Christ does not mean that we get sick because of some sin we have committed, rather, that sin affects our spiritual life in the same way that sickness affects our bodily health. It makes us spiritual cripples. Because Christ was healing people of their physical infirmities, relatives and friends of those who were seriously ill brought their sick to Him wherever He went, hoping for a miraculous cure. One such incident was used by Christ to teach us about sin.

> There the people at once brought to him a paralyzed man lying on a mat. When Jesus saw their faith he said to the paralytic, 'Have courage, son, your sins are forgiven.'
>
> Matthew 9:2

Now some of the scribes of the Jewish faith knew the meaning of what He was saying and it bothered them greatly. They considered this kind of talk blasphemous. They believed that only God could forgive sins and they did not recognize the Divinity of Christ.

> Jesus was aware of what they were thinking and said: 'Why do you harbor evil thoughts? Which is less trouble to say, 'Your sins are forgiven' or 'Stand up and walk?' To help you realize that the Son of Man has authority on earth to forgive sins— he then said to the paralyzed man – 'Stand up! Roll up your mat, and go home.' The man stood up and went toward his home. At the sight, a feeling of awe came over the crowd, and they praised God for giving such authority to men.
>
> Matthew 9:4-8

When Jesus is explaining one of the sacraments to us, He speaks clearly, not in parable. Jesus is teaching us that sin in our lives clouds our vision so that we cannot see truth. We are as blind persons spiritually. Forgiveness of our sins cures our spiritual helplessness and opens our eyes so that we can see truth again.

The forgiveness of our sins is a miraculous occurrence in our lives but we often fail to realize this. It is as momentous as when the paralytic got up and walked. Christ did not perform any miracle for the paralytic that was not given to us at our birth. But just as we may break a bone or contract a disease and lose our physical health, when we commit sin we lose our spiritual health. When this happens we need healing.

Christ knew this and left the means by which we could get this healing. The Sacrament of Confession is God's loving way of relieving us of the terrible burden and the effects of sin. It washes away guilt. It is one of His greatest acts of mercy toward us, His children.

Confession of our sins is our assurance that no matter what happens in our lives, we may ALWAYS remain friends with God if we WILL to do so. We have His Word that His priests can do this for us.

After Christ's resurrection, the apostles were gathered together in a room that they had locked because they were afraid of being caught, accused of being Christians and killed. Christ came to them through the locked door and said to them:

> 'Peace be with you,' he said. When he had said this, he showed them his hands and his side. At the sight of the Lord the disciples rejoiced. 'Peace be with you,' he said again.
> 'As the Father has sent me,
> so I send you.'
> Then he breathed on them and said:
> 'Receive the Holy Spirit.

If you forgive men's sins,
they are forgiven them;
if you hold them bound,
they are held bound.'

John 20:19-23

This is our authority for entering the confessional and confessing our sins to the priest. Confession is the means by which we get the grace to live life as God planned it and to correct ourselves when we fail. Always remember that in the confessional, especially, the priest is God's agent on earth and he will be trying to help you as God would help you.

When the words of absolution are pronounced you are receiving a miracle – your sins are forgiven. You can leave the confessional and never worry about these sins again. Why? Because the priest has forgiven them and they are no longer held bound. That was Christ's promise when He appeared to his apostles. What God forgives, God forgets, so you are now free from all guilt. Even though you might be weak enough to commit this sin again, you will always have the benefit of the confessional to make yourself whole once more.

When your sorrow is real in the confessional you are not a hypocrite if you fail during the week if you are **TRYING** to rid yourself of this particular sin. This is the difference between those who go to confession and **TRY** and those who do not go because they do not really **BELIEVE** their sins will be forgiven.

The Catholic Church provides two ways for its members to receive this sacrament. One is referred to as a private confession because you do not see the priest and the priest cannot not see you. The other type of confession is also private but you sit down in a room with the priest where you can see each other as you talk and pray about your spiritual life. Both ways of confessing our sins are referred to as reconciliation.

Whichever way you choose to receive this sacrament, the end result is that you return to the fullness of God's grace if you were truly sorry for your sins and have a firm intention of changing your life. If you choose to receive this sacrament in the traditional way in the confessional, then you enter the confessional and kneel. As soon as the priest opens the small door that allows him to hear you, you make the Sign of the Cross and say,

Bless me Father, for I have sinned. It has been (however many weeks, months, or years) since my last confession.

Then you tell the priest about any serious sins you have committed and you listen to his advice about how to correct yourself from doing these sins again. You may also tell him about sins in your life which are not serious but about which you want his advice and correction. You may also ask him questions. This is your opportunity to get help from him in a personal way on any matter that may be causing you concern in your spiritual life. It is important to listen carefully to what the priest has to say about the sins in your life. After you and the priest have finished talking, you say:

For these and all the past sins of my life especially those against (mention a particular virtue you have found hard to practice, e.g. charity or purity), I am truly sorry.

The priest may ask you to say the Act of Contrition.

The priest will then give you an appropriate penance to do and you must pay close attention to this part of the confession. It can be very disturbing to you to be so thoughtful of what you were talking about in the confessional that when you leave you have forgotten what the priest said about your penance.

The priest will then absolve you of your sins. Your spiritual life with God has been restored and you are now in His grace. Always remember to thank the priest before you leave the confessional.

You should say or do your penance as quickly as possible after having left the confessional. It is like a debt that you owe God and you will want it repaid promptly.

When you wish to receive this sacrament by talking with the priest face to face, you enter a room that in most parishes is called the Reconciliation Room. In some parishes you now have the option of choosing which kind of confession you prefer immediately on entering the confessional room. This is accomplished by having both a table and a screen in the same room.

The priest will usually begin this type of confession by asking you to pray with him for a good or fruitful confession. The priest will then welcome you to confession and you answer and begin your confession by making the Sign of the Cross and saying it aloud. This signals the fact that your confession is now private and may never be revealed to anyone.

The priest will say a few words of encouragement that will help you have confidence to begin talking about your spiritual life and what may be wrong with it. He may read some appropriate passages from the Bible. The priest will discuss ways to help you in your spiritual life and when your confession is finished he will discuss the manner of your penance for your sins. He may then ask you to express sorrow for your sins in your own words or by the Act of Contrition.

The priest will then absolve your sins while extending his hands over you and you answer, Amen. The priest will conclude your confession by saying: **"The Lord has freed you from your sins. Go in peace." (or something similar).**

When you have received this absolution by either manner of confession, there may not be any outward sign of the inner relief you feel. Yet, when you recognize who God is and what He had to do for the forgiveness of sins, you will be encouraged to try to never sin again. It hurts Him greatly when we do not listen and follow His Commandments. When you make a worthy confession, it is very pleasing to God.

You must realize that there is only one reason why any priest would refuse absolution to you. It is when you **WILLFULLY** refuse to follow God's teachings and His law as expressed through His Commandments and the precepts of His Church. Then you put the priest in the position where he **CANNOT** forgive your sin. Your own persistence in sin prevents it. But the moment you are willing to follow Christ and His teachings, absolution will be happily given to you.

You will be as the prodigal son returning home to his Father who will prepare a banquet for you and welcome you into His house. In the Catholic Church, the priest will say a Mass and give you the Body and Blood of Christ as your welcoming home. These two sacraments are the means by which you can live in a state of grace for the rest of your life.

In the Catholic Church the **PRIEST** is the **ONLY ONE** who can administer the Sacrament of Penance to the faithful. It may be **RECEIVED AS OFTEN AS IT IS NEEDED**.

Through the Sacrament of Penance we receive these benefits:

All sins committed after Baptism are forgiven by a good confession.

Absolution is received and forgiveness completed.

Reconciliation in the fullness of God's grace takes place in our spiritual life.

CONFIRMATION

This sacrament is the bridge between the first three sacraments, and the last three. Baptism, Confession and Holy Communion, are usually received as children. The next two, Matrimony and Holy Orders are received as adults. Anointing of the Sick bestows special graces to all who are suffering illness. (Anointing of the Sick may be administered to a child.)

The sacrament of Confirmation is the beginning of a new life in the Church. It will be a new experience with Christ, a more adult one. The Holy Spirit will make this life possible. The sacraments you received as a child take on a new meaning in your life after Confirmation. You have chosen to enter into membership with a very large group of people in the Catholic, universal church. But it will be through the parish church of your choice that you participate in this organization of the people of God.

Confession and Holy Communion become a sustaining factor in your life as a Christian Catholic. These sacraments should be received frequently if you are to maintain the grace of God in your life. You are growing in body and spirit now and there are many wonderful things about this part of your life but also some fearful ones. You become responsible for so much more now than ever before. Your actions and behavior cannot be blamed on anyone else at this age. You are responsible to God and to yourself for what happens in your life.

Some young people are so fearful of growing up that they decide the decisions they must make are too painful and they refuse the opportunities placed in front of them to help them grow. No longer can you be a Catholic just because your parents are. Now you will face tests of your faith and your parents will not always be there to give you the answers. That is why it is so important for you to study about the Catholic faith before you make the momentous decision to be confirmed.

The sacrament of Confirmation is very much like a graduation. It signals the conclusion of a certain period in your spiritual life and the beginning of a new one. It is unlike a graduation though because there is no certificate certifying that you have completed a course of study. Confirmation is a decision on your part that you want to be an adult Catholic but it does not mean the end of your education in the Catholic faith. That will go on for the rest of your life.

It is hoped that you have had a meaningful **ENCOUNTER WITH CHRIST** before receiving this sacrament. Those who have had this encounter are sure of its experience but cannot explain it to others. We are left speechless in trying to do so because it so very personal. Once we have had this experience our **BELIEF** becomes **KNOWLEDGE**. We **KNOW** Christ is real because we have **MET HIM.** The **GIFT OF FAITH** has been given to us in a way we never knew before. But God chooses the manner and the time when He will impart this gift to us. Until then we may always have doubts.

Christ's disciples had the same doubts that we do. They spoke for us when they asked:

'Lord,' said Thomas, 'we do not know where you are going.
How can we know the way?' Jesus told him:

'I am the way, and the truth, and the life;
no one comes to the Father but through me.
If you really knew me, you would know my Father also.
From this point on you know him; you have seen him.'

'Lord,' Philip said to him, 'show us the Father, and that will be
enough for us.' 'Philip,' Jesus replied, 'after I have been with
you all this time, you still do not know me?
Whoever has seen me has seen the Father.
How can you say, 'Show us the Father?'
Do you not believe that I am in the Father
and the Father is in me?
The words I speak are not spoken of myself;
it is the Father who lives in me accomplishing his works.

Believe me that I am in the Father
and the Father is in me,
or else, believe because of the works I do.
I solemnly assure you,
the man who has faith in me
will do the works I do,
and greater far than these.
Why? Because I go to the Father,
and whatever you ask in my name
I will do,
so as to glorify the Father in the Son.
Anything you ask me in my name
I will do.
If you love me
and obey the commands I give you,
I will ask the Father
and he will give you another Paraclete—
to be with you always:
the Spirit of truth,
whom the world cannot accept,
since it neither sees him nor recognizes him;
but you can recognize him

because he remains with you
and will be within you.

I will not leave you orphaned;
I will come back to you.
A little while now and the world will see me no more:
but you see me
as one who has life, and you will have life.
On that day you will know
that I am in my Father,
and you in me, and I in you.
He who obeys the commandments he has from me
is the man who loves me;
and he who loves me will be loved by my Father.
I too will love him
and reveal myself to him.'

John 14:5-21

No more eloquent or beautiful description of what it means to have faith and to confirm it could be written. Christ speaks to these men as children in the faith and He asks them to mature and believe in Him as adult men. These words are not only for them but for us too.

Judas, another disciple (not Judas Iscariot) questions Jesus further:

'Lord, why is it that you will reveal yourself to us and not to the world?' Jesus answered:

'Anyone who loves me
will be true to my word,
and my Father will love him;
we will come to him
and make our dwelling place with him.

He who does not love me does not keep my words.
Yet the word you hear is not mine;
it comes from the Father who sent me.

This much have I told you while I was still with you;
the Paraclete, the Holy Spirit
whom the Father will send in my name,
will instruct you in everything,
and remind you of all that I told you.

"Peace" is my farewell to you,
my peace is my gift to you;
I do not give it to you as the world gives peace.
Do not be distressed or fearful.
You have heard me say,
"I go away for a while, and I come back to you."
If you truly loved me
you would rejoice to have me go to the Father,
for the Father is greater than I.
I tell you this now, before it takes place,
so that when it takes place you may believe.
I shall not go on speaking to you longer;
the Prince of this world is at hand.
He has no hold on me,
but the world must know that I love the Father
and do as the Father has commanded me.
Come, then! Let us be on our way.

John 14:22-31

Jesus reveals himself fully to his disciples in this meeting. He has lived with his disciples and taught them for a very long time before He had this talk with them. Just as the disciples had to believe in Him at this point, so at confirmation we have to believe also. Christ left earth and returned to His Father so that the Holy Spirit would come.

Now in confirmation we ask the Holy Spirit to come into our lives. We ask for the privilege of believing in Christ. For centuries, billions of people in the world have gone through this experience. The early Christians gave us an example of this:

> When the apostles in Jerusalem heard that Samaria had accepted the word of God, they sent Peter and John to them. The two went down to these people and prayed that they might receive the Holy Spirit. It had not as yet come down upon any of them since they had only been baptized in the name of the Lord Jesus. The pair upon arriving imposed hands on them and they received the Holy Spirit.
>
> Acts 8:14-17

Does this coming of the Holy Spirit into our lives really make a change in them? Again, we have Biblical example through the writings of Paul that it does:

> As Paul laid his hands on them, the Holy Spirit came down on them and they began to speak in tongues and to utter prophecies.
>
> Acts 19:6

Paul further tells us what this confirmation means:

> God is the one who firmly establishes us along with you in Christ; it is he who anointed us and has sealed us, thereby depositing the first payment, the Spirit, in our hearts.
>
> 2 Corinthians 1:21,22

Paul also warns us about the dangers of receiving the Holy Spirit:

> For when men have once been enlightened and have tasted the heavenly gift and become sharers in the Holy Spirit, when they have tasted the good word of God and the powers of the age to come, and then have fallen away, it is impossible to make them repent again, since they are crucifying the Son of God themselves and holding him up to contempt.
>
> Hebrews 6:4-6

This is a terrible warning. It is why it is so important for you to understand what you are doing by being confirmed in this faith. Forever after, you will either give glory or scandal to God. You will either worship Him or crucify Him anew. Once this sacrament has been received it can-

not be undone. Denial of God after having been confirmed in His Church is a serious matter. If you deny Him
afterward it will hurt Him very much. But He is a merciful
God and always provides a way for you to return to Him.

These Scriptures from the Bible link us with the earliest
Christians. But we live in a different day and time. We
must know what we are promising to do with our lives if
we are confirmed in Christ's Church and marked as
Christians with His seal.

WE MUST BELIEVE THAT THE BLESSED TRINITY IS:

Only One God in Three Divine Persons;

The Father, The Son and The Holy Spirit;

**A mystery that we cannot fully understand
but which we must accept by faith in God.**

WE MUST BELIEVE THAT GOD THE FATHER, IS:

The First Person of the Blessed Trinity;

The Creator of all things;

**The Father who sent His only Son to redeem
us by His death;**

**The Heavenly Father who protects and cares
for us at all times and in every circumstance
through our life on earth.**

WE MUST BELIEVE THAT JESUS CHRIST IS:

The Second Person of the Blessed Trinity;

The only begotten Son of God;

Both God and man;

The Son of God whose Mother was the Virgin Mary who conceived Him by the power of the Holy Spirit, not man;

The Son of God whose foster-father was Joseph, and His guardian

WE MUST BELIEVE THAT THE HOLY SPIRIT IS:

The Third Person of the Blessed Trinity;

The Spirit of truth who proceeds from the Father and the Son;

The Advocate who bears witness that Christ is the Son of God.

WE MUST BELIEVE THAT JESUS CHRIST SAVED US BY:

Dying on the cross in atonement to God for our sins;

Founding the Church to continue His life with us on earth;

Leaving the sacraments to help sustain us in our spiritual lives until He comes for us.

WE MUST BELIEVE THAT THE CATHOLIC CHURCH IS A LIVING COMMUNITY OF:

All baptized persons united in the true faith as taught by Jesus Christ through the prophets, His apostles and disciples;

All of the family of God celebrating the same sacrifice of the Mass;

All of the family of God receiving the same sacraments;

All of the family of God led by the Pope.

WE MUST BELIEVE THAT THE CATHOLIC CHURCH GETS
ITS AUTHORITY TO TEACH FROM:

Its founder, Jesus Christ;

**The bishops who were given their authority
by Christ;**

**The promise of Christ never to let the gates
of hell prevail against His Church;**

**The promise of Christ to keep the doctrines
of His Church affecting our faith and morals infallible (free from error).**

WE MUST BELIEVE THAT THE RESURRECTION OF
JESUS CHRIST AND HIS ASCENSION INTO HEAVEN
MEANS:

**That He arose by His own power from the tomb of
death on Easter Sunday;**

**That He walked, talked and ate with His friends for
forty days after this resurrection so that we would
have living proof by these witnesses of His rising
from the dead;**

**That He ascended into heaven after forty days
to return to the Father.**

WE MUST BELIEVE THAT WHEN WE DIE IT IS:

The end of our life on earth;

**The beginning of a new existence which will
be eternal;**

**The time when faithfulness to God will mean that
this new existence will be lived with Him in a place
of endless joy;**

The time when unfaithfulness to God will mean this new existence will be lived in a place where we suffer the loss of God forever;

The time when our bodies, though dead, will someday be reunited with our souls to be in glory just as Jesus and Mary are now.

WE MUST BELIEVE THAT THE APOSTLES ARE:

The twelve original followers of Christ chosen by Him;

Those on whom Jesus bestowed powers of priesthood at the Last Supper;

Peter, whom Christ chose to be first among all of the apostles, and the rock on whom He built his Church for His people;

WE MUST BELIEVE THAT THE SUCCESSORS OF THE APOSTLES ARE:

All of the Popes since Peter;

All of the bishops and priests

WE MUST BELIEVE IN GRACE AND THAT IT IS:

A gift from God obtained through the merits of Jesus and given to us in three ways:

SANCTIFYING GRACE:

A free gift from God given at Baptism that makes us adopted children of God, a temple of the Holy Spirit, and a holy and pleasing person to God.

ACTUAL GRACE:

A special help from God when we need it.

SACRAMENTAL GRACE:

A special help from God promised when we receive each sacrament.

WE MUST BELIEVE THAT PRAYER IS:

Talking to God;

The Mass,(when properly said, a perfect prayer);

Those times when we talk to God from our hearts;

An affirmation that we believe in God and that He can give us what we pray for because He told us He would;

The way that we glorify God and worship Him.

WE MUST BELIEVE IN THE NECESSITY OF PRAYER BECAUSE:

Jesus taught us to pray by His example;

Jesus taught us to ask anything of our heavenly Father in His name;

It acknowledges our dependence on God;

It provides us with a means of communicating with Him at all times and under all circumstances.

As you read over what Catholics must believe in order to be a practicing member of the Church you will see that all of these beliefs are contained in the Nicene (or Apostles') Creed. It is important for you to think about all of this in order for you to decide whether or not you want to be confirmed in this faith and live your life in accordance with these beliefs.

By asking to receive the Sacrament of Confirmation, you will be promising to live a special kind of life consecrated to God in all you do. This Creed, therefore, becomes very important in your daily life. But you must remember that your faith and the practice of it will be tested many times in your life. How you have answered these questions will determine whether or not you have the necessary commitment to fulfill your duties as a defender of the faith.

Do not be foolish enough to think that this is easy. It is not. It takes a lot of courage to be a Catholic and defend what Christ has taught. Christ spoke clearly to us of this in the Gospel of St. John in the 15th, 16th and 17th Chapters. If you read these you will see that while you make promises to Christ with your life, He, too, makes beautiful promises to you which are marvelous.

If you wish to be confirmed in this faith, there are three things you must do.

**Express your desire to be confirmed
to your parish priest.**

**Choose a sponsor of the same sex who
is a practicing Catholic.**

**Choose a new name (one of the saints
of the Church).**

The Church treats this sacrament in a very special way because it is such an important one. **A BISHOP** or **ARCH-BISHOP** will be the one to administer the sacrament of Confirmation. There is only one other time when a bishop or archbishop must administer a sacrament and that is at the ordination of men to the priesthood (Holy Orders).

During the Confirmation ceremony you will be anointed with **HOLY CHRISM**. Holy Chrism is oil that has been blessed by the bishop or archbishop on Holy Thursday. It is a mixture of olive oil and perfume called balm. The reason that you are being anointed is that you are being set apart for God and the oil represents the spiritual anointing of the Holy Spirit who comes to you in Confirmation. Kings of old (like David and Solomon) were anointed with oil to set them apart from other men, for God. It also means that just as kings (like Christ) must serve their people, now you must become a servant of others for Christ. Before His Crucifixion, Mary Magdalene anointed Christ with oil and balm.

Your sponsor will affirm to other members of the Church that you are worthy of Confirmation.

Your sponsor, then, should be your spiritual guardian and should try to help you live up to the promises you will be making and pray for your spiritual welfare. Your sponsor has an obligation to give you good example in his or her life. You should keep all of this in mind when choosing this person.

You must also choose a new name and it should be the name of a Christian saint whom you especially admire and with whom you can have a special relationship in your prayers. This saint can become a very important friend in your spiritual life if you will allow the friendship to develop. Your new saint friend is already in heaven with Jesus and can intercede with Him for you. The Church teaches us that our chosen saint will watch over us and guard us in times of temptation because the promises you make will be difficult to keep.

After you have expressed your desire to be confirmed, chosen your sponsor and your new name, the Church then agrees to confirm you in a special ceremony. During the ceremony there will usually be a Mass at which the Bishop or Archbishop presides. At some time during the

Mass, both you and your sponsor will be asked to renew your baptismal vows for a very special reason. What was promised for you at baptism will now be repeated so that you may now give your willing consent. You and your sponsor will be asked to:

Reject Satan and all his works;

Believe in God, the Father, in Jesus Christ, the Son, and in the Holy Spirit;

Believe in the Catholic Church as the true faith.

At an appointed time during the Mass you and your sponsor will approach the altar. The bishop or archbishop will dip his thumb into sacred chrism and he will trace the Sign of the Cross on your forehead and say:

"(Your chosen name. e.g., Mary,) receive the seal of the Holy Spirit, the gift of the Father. Peace be with you."You will answer, "And also with you."

You will then stand up and a priest will wipe the sacred chrism from your forehead (it is sacred and your spiritual anointing has already taken place) and you and your sponsor will return to your pews.

The seal of the Holy Spirit is on you and will remain with you always. There will be an increase of sanctifying grace in your life and you will always have the strength to be a "witness" for Christ if you will call upon the Holy Spirit for it.

You are now a very special person in the life of God and His Church.

MATRIMONY

The sacrament of Matrimony in the Catholic Church is the coming together of a man and a woman who wish to express their desire before God to be transformed into a new life as husband and wife with His blessing. They come to His Church to make their vows to one another before Him. These vows bind them as husband and wife for the rest of their lives. God blesses their union and they become a new family unit in the Church. Through their union they and God may bring new life into the world. The couple is then mother and father as well as husband and wife.

Each and every sacramental marriage must be open to receiving children if God chooses to send them to the couple. Therefore, matrimony is the taking on of a SACRIFICAL kind of life for God. Just as God offered His life for His people and His Church, a man and woman who marry give up their lives for each other and their children. Not every person is capable or desirous of this kind of sacrifice. Therefore, this sacrament is reserved for those who are mature enough to make the commitment necessary to live this kind of life.

Marriage is the means by which God has chosen to bring new life into the world and into His Church. For those who love each other and God enough to be willing to accept the burdens that sacramental marriage brings, God makes beautiful promises to them in return for their sacrifice of love. The greatest promise is that He will provide the kind of special loving care that will sustain and help them through whatever difficulties they may confront in trying to be faithful to each other and to Him throughout their marriage to each other. God, blessing and caring for His people, is recorded in the earliest Chapter of the Old Testament:

God blessed them, saying: 'Be fertile and multiply; fill the earth and subdue it. Have dominion over the fish of the sea, the birds of the air, and all the living things that move on the earth.' God also said: 'See, I give you every seed-bearing plant all over the earth and every tree that has seed-bearing fruit on it to be your food; and to all the animals of the land, all the birds of the air, and all the living creatures that crawl on the ground, I give all the green plants for food.' And so it happened. God looked at everything he had made, and he found it very good.

Genesis 1:28-31

What a blessing for mankind! What an inheritance from a loving Father. The marriage of our first parents was just as lovingly blessed:

The LORD God then took the man and settled him in the garden of Eden, to cultivate and care for it. The LORD God gave man this order: 'You are free to eat from any of the trees of the garden except the tree of knowledge of good and bad. From that tree you shall not eat; the moment you eat from it you are surely doomed to die.'

The LORD God said: 'It is not good for the man to be alone. I will make a suitable partner for him.' So the LORD God formed out of the ground various wild animals and various birds of the air, and he brought them to the man to see what he would call them; whatever the man called each of them would be its name. The man gave names to all the cattle, all the birds of the air, and all the wild animals; but none proved to be the suitable partner for the man.

So, the LORD God cast a deep sleep on the man, and while he was asleep, he took out one of his ribs and closed up its place with flesh. The LORD God then built up into a woman the rib that he had taken from the man. When he brought her to the man, the man said:
'This one, at last, is bone of my bones
and flesh of my flesh;

> This one shall be called 'woman,'
> for out of 'her man' this one has been taken.'
>
> That is why a man leaves his father and mother and clings
> to his wife, and the two of them become one body.
>
> The man and his wife were both naked, yet they felt no
> shame.
>
> *Genesis 2:15-25*

This is the life God planned for His people. He wanted them to have a beautiful life in every respect. It is only when sin enters the life of man that it becomes distorted.

> Now the serpent was the most cunning of all the animals that
> the LORD God had made. The serpent asked the woman,
> 'Did God really tell you not to eat from any of the trees in the
> garden?' The woman answered the serpent: 'We may eat of
> the fruit of the trees in the garden; it is only about the fruit of
> the tree in the middle of the garden that God said, 'You shall
> not eat it or even touch it, lest you die.' But the serpent said
> to the woman: 'You certainly will not die! No, God knows well
> that the moment you eat of it your eyes will be opened and
> you will be like gods who know what is good and what is bad.'
> The woman saw that the tree was good for food, pleasing to
> the eyes, and desirable for gaining wisdom. So she took
> some of its fruit and ate it; and she also gave some to her
> husband, who was with her, and he ate it. Then the eyes of
> both of them were opened, and they realized that they were
> naked; so they sewed fig leaves together and made loincloths
> for themselves.
>
> *Genesis 3:1-7*

God had given the first commandment to Adam and Eve. You shall not eat of the fruit of this tree. They both decided NOT TO OBEY. Sin was for them the same as it has been for all men of all time, delightful to behold, but oh, so deadly.

The serpent lied. They did die. But even in their sinful
condition God did not abandon them, nor will He abandon us. When Adam and Eve disobeyed God's command,
they hid themselves from the face of God because of fear
and He said to them:

> The LORD God then called to the man and asked him,
> 'Where are you?' He answered, 'I heard you in the garden;
> but I was afraid, because I was naked, so I hid myself.' Then
> he asked, 'Who told you that you were naked? You have
> eaten, then, from the tree of which I had forbidden you to
> eat!' The man replied, 'The woman whom you put here with
> me – she gave me fruit from the tree, and so I ate it.' The
> LORD God then asked the woman, 'Why did you do such a
> thing?' The woman answered, 'The serpent tricked me into it,
> so I ate it.'
>
> *Genesis 3:9-13*

God then curses the serpent that tempted them and He
is angry that they have disobeyed Him. He punishes
them but He does not leave them in their sorrowful state.

> For the man and his wife the LORD God made leather gar-
> ments, with which he clothed them.
>
> *Genesis 3:21*

This is the first recorded shedding of blood for the atonement of sin. It is to be repeated over and over again
throughout the Old Testament until the coming of Christ.

> The man had relations with his wife Eve, and she conceived
> and bore Cain, saying, 'I have produced a man with the help
> of the LORD.'
>
> *Genesis 4:1*

The coming together of a man and a woman in marriage
has thus been blessed from the beginning of mankind.
Christ affirms this blessing in the New Testament.

Have you not read that at the beginning the Creator made them male and female and declared, 'For this reason a man shall leave his father and mother and cling to his wife, and the two shall become as one'? Thus they are no longer two but one flesh. Therefore, let no man separate what God has joined.

Matthew 19:4-6

Christ performed His first recorded miracle at a marriage feast in Cana. It was at the request of His mother, Mary, that He declared Himself to the world and began His public ministry. At this marriage feast Jesus is fulfilling the promise of God to always sustain married couples in their married lives. This was not a miracle of necessity or of healing that Christ performed. Rather it was one of loving concern for His mother and her friends and the couple who were celebrating this occasion.

It is Mary who comes to Him in behalf of her friends who are not going to have enough wine for all of the guests at this wedding feast. (In those days the celebration could go on for days.)

At a certain point the wine ran out, and Jesus' mother told him, 'They have no more wine.' Jesus replied, 'Woman, how does this concern of yours involve me? My hour has not yet come.' His mother instructed those waiting on table, 'DO WHATEVER HE TELLS YOU.'

As prescribed for Jewish ceremonial washings, there were at hand six stone water jars, each one holding fifteen to twenty-five gallons. 'Fill those jars with water,' Jesus ordered, at which they filled them to the brim. 'Now,' he said, 'draw some out and take it to the waiter in charge.' They did as he instructed them. The waiter in charge tasted the water made wine, without knowing where it had come from; only the waiters knew, since they had drawn the water. Then the waiter in charged called the groom over and remarked to him: 'People usually serve the choice wine first; then when the guests have been drinking awhile, a lesser vintage. What you have done is keep the choice wine until now.' Jesus performed this first of his signs at Cana in Galilee. Thus did he reveal his glory, and his disciples believed in him.

John 2:3-11

At this marriage feast Mary speaks for one of the few times when her words are recorded. "Do whatever he tells you." With these few words Mary has told all married couples who ask her Son's blessing on their marriage how to have a feast all of their married life. Christ not only provided wine for this wedding but it was of the finest vintage.

Jesus warns us in the New Testament about keeping God's commandments regarding marriage: He told them,

'Whoever divorces his wife and marries another commits adultery against her; and the woman who divorces her husband and marries another commits adultery.'

Mark 10:11,12

The Scriptures are literally filled with explanations of what it means to be married; how husband and wife should regard one another. St. Paul is prolific in his discussions about married life and how married couples are to treat one another.

Wives should be submissive to their husbands as if to the Lord because the husband is head of his wife just as Christ is head of his body the church, as well as its savior. As the church submits to Christ, so wives should submit to their husbands in everything.

Husbands, love your wives, as Christ loved the church. He gave himself up for her to make her holy, purifying her in the bath of water by the power of the word, to present to himself a glorious church, holy and immaculate, without stain or wrinkle or anything of that sort. Husbands should love their wives as they do their own bodies. He who loves his wife loves himself. Observe that no one ever hates his own flesh; no, he nourishes it and takes care of it as Christ cares for the church—for we are members of his body.

'For this reason a man shall leave his father and mother,
and shall cling to his wife,
and the two shall be made into one.'

This is a great foreshadowing; I mean that it refers to Christ
and the Church. In any case, each one should love his wife
as he loves himself, the wife for her part showing respect for
her husband.

Ephesians 5:22-32

(See also 1 *Corinthians* 7:1-7 *and Romans* 7:2-6)

One of the most beautiful accounts of God's loving care
for married couples who are faithful to Him is in the Book
of Tobit in the Old Testament. The angel Raphael is sent
by God to a couple to help them through all of their trou-
bles. It is well worth reading.

St. Peter, our first Pope, spoke on marriage:

You married women must obey your husbands, so that any of
them who do not believe in the word of the gospel may be
won over apart from preaching, through their wives' conduct.
They have only to observe the reverent purity of your way of
life. The affectation of an elaborate hairdress, the wearing of
golden jewelry, or the donning of rich robes is not for you.
Your adornment is rather the hidden character of the heart,
expressed in the unfading beauty of a calm and gentle dispo-
sition. This is precious in God's eyes. The holy women of past
ages used to adorn themselves in this way, reliant on God
and obedient to their husbands – for example, Sarah, who
was subject to Abraham and called him her master. You are
her children when you do what is right and let no fears alarm
you.

You husbands, too, must show consideration for those who
share your lives. Treat women with respect as the weaker
sex, heirs just as much as you to the gracious gift of life.
If you do so, nothing will keep your prayers from being
answered.

1 *Peter* 3:1-6

The sacrament of Matrimony is administered in the Catholic Church in a beautiful ceremony wherein the bride and groom come together before God in His Church in the midst of their invited friends and guests. The kind of love that causes a man and woman to decide to marry and spend their lives together is such a wonderful and powerful kind of love that all of the relatives and friends who know and love them will want to celebrate this occasion with them.

Before they can partake of this ceremony, however, they must go to God's priest and ask to receive His blessing on their marriage. The priest will counsel the couple to try to make sure they understand the commitments they are making to each other and the Church.

Each couple must realize that they are more than confirmed Catholics when they marry. They now ask for the privilege of loving each other in the most total way that is known to mankind. In loving each other this way, new life may be brought into the world for them to nurture and love. The priest must make sure they are willing to commit themselves to the joys and sorrows that marriage will bring into their lives. They are asking to enter one of the most difficult vocations in the world. Therefore, God's blessing cannot be lightly or easily given.

There is one great difference in the sacrament of Matrimony from all other sacraments. It is the only sacrament **NOT** administered by the priest or bishop. It is the **COUPLE BEING MARRIED WHO ADMINISTER IT TO EACH OTHER**. The priest does bring them God's blessing and assists them in their marriage ceremony but it is the couple who consecrate themselves to each other for life. The death of one of the marriage partners can cause this sacrament to be received again if the living partner should want to marry another person.

HOLY ORDERS

The sacrament of Holy Orders in the Catholic Church is the ordination of men to the priesthood whom God has chosen. "Holy" means sacred and "Orders" means command. Therefore Holy Orders is a sacred command from God that a man give up the kind of life that other men have and follow Him to serve the people of God in His Church. Men do not choose God in order to become priests. **HE CHOOSES THEM**.

The priests are the shepherds of the people in their spiritual lives. For this reason they are very special persons in the functions they perform for the sake of Christ. It is because all of the sacraments of the Church are dependent on this one that we should have a good understanding of what it really means to be called by God to become a priest in His Church.

From the beginning God used very special people to do important work for Him for the benefit of His people. Throughout the Old Testament there are men such as Adam, Noah, Abraham, Isaac, Jacob, Moses, Nathan, Daniel, David, Solomon, Jeremiah, Ezekiel, Isaiah, and many others, especially called to do His will for the purpose of helping His people in their lives on earth.

In the New Testament, John the Baptist was ORDAINED to be the messenger of the Word of God and His coming. Many times these men were afraid and pleaded with God not to ask them to do the things He wanted them to do. But God promised to be with them and give them all the help they needed to do His work. Abraham was an outstanding example of a man who listened to God and believed in Him faithfully.

While Christ was on earth **HE CHOSE** twelve apostles to follow Him and learn how to do His will and teach others to do it also. These men gave up their lives to follow Jesus and become a new kind of man, completely transformed to preaching the gospel of Christ and bringing His life to His people through the New Covenant that Christ would institute at the Last Supper. Christ ordained these men as the new shepherds of His people replacing the former prophets and messengers God had sent from the beginning. Ever since Christ came to earth, men have been ordained to the priesthood because they were chosen by God and were willing to follow His call just as the twelve apostles did.

Of all of the sacraments, the priesthood is written about the most in Holy Scripture. In the Old Testament there are many accounts of blood sacrifices to God in atonement of sin. When Adam and Eve had sinned their eyes were opened to their nakedness and they made fig leaves with which to cover themselves. But fig leaves soon dry up and wither.

It was God who provided the means by which they could cover themselves – through a blood sacrifice – as He killed animals and made for them garments from their skin. And on and on throughout the Old Testament is the renewal of the blood sacrifice in atonement of sin. This was the foretelling of the blood sacrifice that Christ would finally make for all of the sins of mankind for all time. The manner in which this sacrifice continues to be made is through His priests offering of the Holy Sacrifice of the Mass.

What kind of men must they be? They must be **OTHER CHRISTS.**

Every high priest is taken from among men and made their representative before God, to offer gifts and sacrifices for sins. He is able to deal patiently with erring sinners, for he himself is beset by weakness and so must make sin offerings for himself as well as for the people. One does not take this

honor on his own initiative, but only when called by God as
Aaron was. Even Christ did not glorify himself with the office
of high priest; he received it from the One who said to him,

> 'You are my son;
> today I have begotten you';
> just as he says in another place,
> 'You are a priest forever,
> according to the order of Melchizedek.'
>
> In the days when he was in the flesh, he offered prayers and
> supplications with loud cries and tears to God, who was able
> to save him from death, and he was heard because of his
> reverence. Son though he was, he learned obedience from
> what he suffered; and when perfected, he became the source
> of eternal salvation for all who obey him, designated by God
> as high priest according to the order of Melchizedek.
>
> *Hebrews 5:1-10*

Melchizedek is mentioned twice in this account. He is
important in the history of the Eucharist as he was the
only one in the Old Testament accounts to have used
bread and wine as a sacrifice. The account of this is in
Genesis. Abraham is returning to his home after having
saved his brother, Lot, and his family from capture and
enslavement:

> When Abram returned from his victory over Chedorlaomer
> and the kings who were allied with him, the king of Sodom
> went out to greet him in the valley of Shaveh (that is, the
> King's Valley).
>
> Melchizedek, king of Salem, brought out bread and wine, and
> being a priest of God Most High, he blessed Abram with
> these words:
>
> 'Blessed be Abram by God Most High,
> the creator of heaven and earth;

And blessed be God Most High,
who delivered your foes into your hand.'

Then Abram gave him a tenth of everything.

Genesis 14:17-20

When Christ called His disciples, Simon and Andrew,
James and John:

Jesus said to them, 'Come after me; I will make you fishers of
men.'

Mark 1:17

The prophet Jeremiah in the Old Testament foretold this
event in these words:

Look! I will send many fishermen, says the LORD, to catch
them.

Jeremiah 16:16

The apostles were chosen from among Christ's
disciples:

Then he went out to the mountain to pray, spending the night
in communion with God. At daybreak he called his disciples
and selected twelve of them to be his apostles: Simon, to
whom he gave the name Peter, and Andrew his brother,
James and John, Philip and Bartholomew, Matthew and
Thomas, James son of Alphaeus, and Simon called the
Zealot, Judas son of James, and Judas Iscariot, who turned
traitor.

Luke 6:12-16

It is only after Christ had spent the night in prayer with
His heavenly Father that He chose these twelve. After
these were chosen, Christ began to teach them and show
them the manner in which they were to go forth and
preach His gospel and He gave them special powers to
do His will.

> Jesus summoned the Twelve and began to send them out two by two, giving them authority over unclean spirits. He instructed them to take nothing on the journey but a walking stick – no food, no traveling bag, not a coin in the purses in their belts. They were, however, to wear sandals. 'Do not bring a second tunic,' he said, and added: 'Whatever house you find yourself in, stay there until you leave the locality. If any place will not receive you or hear you, shake its dust from your feet in testimony against them as you leave.' With that they went off, preaching the need of repentance. They expelled many demons, anointed the sick with oil, and worked many cures.
>
> *Mark 6:7-13*

Christ is now sending forth His CHOSEN ONES to do His will in teaching of Him and His Divinity. Notice how wrathful His punishment is on those who will not hear His Word.

The scribes and Pharisees of the Jewish faith are scandalized by His action and chide Him for the manner in which He teaches His apostles. Christ rebukes them with the prophesy of Isaiah concerning them:

> 'Why do your disciples not follow the tradition of our ancestors, but instead take food without purifying their hands?'
> He said to them:
>
> 'How accurately Isaiah prophesied about you hypocrites when he wrote,
>
> "This people pays me lip service
> but their heart is far from me.
>
> Empty is the reverence they do me
> because they teach as dogmas mere human precepts."'
>
> *Mark 7:5-7*

Christ continues His angry rebuke while the apostles are listening.

'You disregard God's commandment and cling to what is
human tradition.'

He went on to say: 'You have made a fine art of setting aside
God's commandment in the interests of keeping your traditions! For example, Moses said, "Honor your father and your
mother"; and in another place, "Whoever curses father or
mother shall be put to death." Yet you declare, "If a person
says to his father or mother, Any support you might have had
from me is **korban**" (that is, dedicated to God), you allow him
to do nothing more for his father or mother. That is the way
you nullify God's word in favor of the traditions you have
handed on. And you have many other such practices
besides.' He summoned the crowd again and said to them:
'Hear me, all of you, and try to understand. Nothing that
enters a man from outside can make him impure; that which
comes out of him, and only that, constitutes impurity. Let
everyone heed what he hears!'

Mark 7:8-16

The apostles do not fully understand what Christ is saying and they question Him about it. Christ is now taking
on the work of teaching these men about the new Church
that He will establish and He tells them His meaning
clearly:

When he got home, away from the crowd, his disciples questioned him about the proverb. 'Are you, too, incapable of
understanding?' he asked them. 'Do you not see that nothing
that enters a man from outside can make him impure? It does
not penetrate his being, but enters his stomach only and
passes into the latrine.' Thus did he render all foods clean.
He went on: 'What emerges from within a man, that and nothing else is what makes him impure. Wicked designs come
from the deep recesses of the heart: acts of fornication, theft,
murder, adulterous conduct, greed, maliciousness, deceit,
sensuality, envy, blasphemy, arrogance, an obtuse spirit.
All these evils come from within and render a man impure.'

Mark 7:17-23

Christ began to teach these new apostles of the Church and begin their journey to the priesthood. He poignantly describes what it means to be a priest when He asks Peter if he loves Him:

> When they had eaten their meal, Jesus said to Simon Peter, 'Simon, son of John, do you love me more than these?' 'Yes, Lord,' he said, 'you know that I love you.' At which Jesus said, 'Feed my lambs.'
>
> A second time, he put his question, 'Simon, son of John, do you love me?' 'Yes, Lord,' Peter said, 'you know that I love you.' Jesus replied, 'Tend my sheep.'
>
> A third time Jesus asked him, 'Simon, son of John, do you love me?' Peter was hurt because he had asked a third time, 'Do you love me?' So he said to him: 'Lord you know everything. You know well that I love you.' Jesus said to him, 'Feed my sheep.
> I tell you solemnly:
> as a young man
> you fastened your belt
> and went about as you pleased;
> but when you are older
> you will stretch out your hands,
> and another will tie you fast
> and carry you off against your will.'
>
> (What he said indicated the sort of death by which Peter was to glorify God.) When Jesus had finished speaking he said to him, 'Follow me.'
>
> *John 21:15-19*

Christ was telling Peter the manner of life and the cruel death that he would suffer. But He speaks to more than Peter – to all priests. His invitation is to "Follow Me" to the sacrament of Holy Orders. He makes it plain that their life will not be an easy one. They will suffer much on account of His calling them. But, oh, what a reward they will have!

St. Paul talks about the priesthood in his letters to Timothy in 2 Timothy 1, 2, 3, and 4. He describes the life of a priest in great detail:

> For this reason, I remind you to stir into flame the gift of God bestowed when my hands were laid on you. The Spirit God has given us is no cowardly spirit, but rather one that makes us strong, loving and wise. Therefore, never be ashamed of your testimony to our Lord, nor of me, a prisoner for his sake; but with the strength which comes from God bear your share of the hardship which the gospel entails.

> God has saved us and has called us to a holy life, not because of any merit of ours but according to his own design – the grace held out to us in Christ Jesus before the world began but now made manifest through the appearance of our Savior. He has robbed death of its power and has brought life and immortality into clear light through the gospel. In the service of this gospel I have been appointed preacher and apostle and teacher, and for its sake I undergo present hardships. But I am not ashamed, for I know him in whom I have believed, and I am confident that he is able to guard what has been entrusted to me until that Day. Take as a model of sound teaching what you have heard me say, in faith and love in Christ Jesus. Guard the rich deposit of faith with the help of the Holy Spirit who dwells within us.

> *2 Timothy 1:6-14*

> Bear hardship along with me as a good soldier of Christ Jesus.

> *2 Timothy 2:3*

> Similarly, if one takes part in an athletic contest, he cannot receive the winner's crown unless he has kept the rules.

> *2 Timothy 2:5*

You can depend on this:

If we have died with him
we shall also live with him;
If we hold out to the end
we shall also reign with him.
But if we deny him he will deny us.
If we are unfaithful he will still remain faithful,
for he cannot deny himself.

2 Timothy 2: 11-13

In the presence of God and of Christ Jesus, who is coming to
judge the living and the dead, and by his appearing and his
kingly power, I charge you to preach the word, to stay with
this task whether convenient or inconvenient – correcting,
reproving, appealing – constantly teaching and never losing
patience. For the time will come when people will not tolerate
sound doctrine, but, following their own desires, will surround
themselves with teachers who tickle their ears. They will stop
listening to the truth and will wander off to fables. As for you,
be steady and self-possessed; put up with hardship, perform
your work as an evangelist, fulfill your ministry.

I for my part am already being poured out like a libation. The
time of my dissolution is near. I have fought the good fight,
I have finished the race, I have kept the faith. From now on a
merited crown awaits me; on that Day the Lord, just judge
that he is, will award it to me – and not only to me, but to all
who have looked for his appearing with eager longing.

2 Timothy 4:1-8

St. Paul is eloquent in his praise of the priestly life
though he acknowledges that it is a very hard life. Priests
willingly take on this sacrificial life and become as Christ
bringing us His saving grace through His sacraments.
This is their principal function, along with teaching and
preaching the gospel of Christ wherever they can and

continually spreading the seed of the Word of God all their lives. Our first Pope, the apostle Peter, speaks about the ministry:

> To the elders among you I, a fellow elder, a witness of Christ's suffering and sharer in the glory that is to be revealed, make this appeal. God's flock is in your midst; give it a shepherd's care. Watch over it willingly as God would have you do, not under constraint; and not for shameful profit either, but generously. Be examples to the flock, not lording it over those assigned to you, so that when the chief Shepherd appears you will win for yourselves the unfading crown of glory.
>
> 1 Peter 5:1-4

A **BISHOP** or **ARCHBISHOP** administers the sacrament of Holy Orders at a very special ceremony in the Church. The bishop or archbishop is the **ONLY ONE** who can confer this sacrament on men. Each man so chosen must willingly consent to serve Christ and then the sacrament is administered only after they have spent many years of study in a theological seminary. The sacrament of Holy Orders can be received **ONLY ONCE**. They are **FOREVER**, even unto eternity.

HOLY ORDERS ARE:

A priest serving God and His people by preaching the gospel;

A priest serving God and His people by administering the sacraments;

A priest serving God and His people by exercising the teaching authority of the Church.

ANOINTING OF THE SICK

This sacrament is probably the most misunderstood of all the sacraments of the Church. It has been known as Extreme Unction sometimes referred to as "The Last Rites". Many members of the Church believe it is a last blessing before death. This is easy to understand when we think about the fact that it is a sacrament given to people who are seriously ill. Many people die after having received it. On the other hand, it is a **HEALING SACRAMENT**. Properly understood, it is a sacrament of hope.

The healing power in this sacrament has a two-fold purpose: To **HEAL THE BODY** and to **HEAL THE SOUL**, or spirit. In this respect it is very closely linked with the sacraments of spiritual life, Confession and Holy Communion. Both may be received during this anointing. What we hope for in this sacrament is a healing of the body and that is a miraculous effect. If we understand that ALL of the sacraments have a miraculous quality about them, it is not so difficult to believe that a miracle occurs in this one too.

Christ used the healing of the sick as a demonstration of his miraculous healing power over the soul because the body is something we can see, whereas the spirit is not. The meaning of Extreme Unction is the bringing forth of an extraordinary sacred fervor. It is a very special consecration; a gush of spiritual awareness and dependence made possible by illness. It is an anointing with sacred oil of the body and a deliverance of the soul from all effects of sins through intense prayer.

When our bodies become seriously ill there is always the danger of death being imminent. It is a signal that we are in immediate danger. All of us are going to die. We know this but avoid thinking about it because death is such an unknown factor in our lives and we do not know the time of our death. If our bodies are healthy and we are young, we tend to think that death is a long way off. Yet, it may not be so. The young also die.

When our bodies become seriously ill, the Church can apply its healing power to the body and the spirit. Christ knew our human condition and left this sacrament for us because He knew we might put off our spiritual welfare until the last moment. It is another way He provides for us with loving care. He wants us to have the benefit of heaven with Him.

When we receive this sacrament, we may not be cured in body but we shall certainly experience a forgiveness of sin that will bring grace to our soul and protect it for heaven should we die. When we see someone who has lost their bodily health, we feel very sorry for them because we know what they have lost. The loss of spiritual health is not so easily seen and as a result we are not so concerned. Yet which is more important? Sin does to the soul what disease and injuries do to the body. This is a concept that is very hard for most of us to understand and appreciate.

This sacrament comes into our lives at a time when this realization comes into sharp focus. Christ spoke to two sinners who were certainly in need of healing while He was hanging on the cross with death imminent to all three of them. One wanted Him to take him down from his cross and believed that would heal his body. The other asked for spiritual healing and gained heaven!

One of the criminals hanging in crucifixion blasphemed Him:

'Aren't you the Messiah? Then save yourself and us.' But the other one rebuked him: 'Have you no fear of God, seeing you

> are under the same sentence? We deserve it, after all. We
> are only paying the price for what we've done, but this man
> has done nothing wrong.' He then said, *'Jesus, remember me*
> *when you enter upon your reign.'* And Jesus replied, 'I assure
> you: this day you will be with me in paradise.'
>
> Luke 23:39-43

The good thief was anointed while on the cross! If ever
there was a vivid example of the difference between spiritual and physical healing, this is it. The good thief was
not released from his physical cross but he attained
heaven. The other thief remained in his sinful state
because he would not ask for spiritual healing.

Through anointing of the sick God's peace is brought into
our lives even though we may be left with the physical
effects of ill health. Christ used physical healing to con-
vince us of His Divinity. It was through the use of this
power that Christ answered John the Baptist's question.

> Now John in prison heard about the works Christ was per-
> forming, and sent a message by his disciples to ask him,
> 'Are you "He who is to come" or do we look for another?' In
> reply, Jesus said to them: 'Go back and report to John what
> you hear and see: the blind recover their sight, cripples walk,
> lepers are cured, the deaf hear, dead men are raised to life,
> and the poor have the good news preached to them. Blest is
> the man who finds no stumbling block in me.'
>
> Matthew 11:2-6

See the works that Christ does and believe in Him. Many
did when He walked the earth. Many of them were so anx-
ious to have this miraculous power used in behalf of
themselves or their loved ones that they went to extraordinary means to try to receive the attention of Christ.

> He came back to Capernaum after a lapse of several days
> and word got around that he was at home. At that they began
> to gather in great numbers. There was no longer any room for
> them, even around the door. While he was delivering God's

word to them, some people arrived bringing a paralyzed man to him. The four who carried him were unable to bring him to Jesus because of the crowd, so they began to open up the roof over the spot where Jesus was. When they had made a hole, they let down the mat on which the paralytic was lying. When Jesus saw their faith, he said to the paralyzed man, 'My son, your sins are forgiven.' Now some of the scribes were sitting there asking themselves: 'Why does the man talk in that way? He commits blasphemy! Who can forgive sins except God alone?' Jesus was immediately aware of their reasoning, though they kept it to themselves, and he said to them: 'Why do you harbor these thoughts? Which is easier to say to the paralytic, "Your sins are forgiven," or to say, "Stand up, pick up your mat, and walk again"? That you may know that the Son of Man has authority on earth to forgive sins' (he said to the paralyzed man), 'I command you: Stand up! Pick up your mat and go home.' The man stood and picked up his mat and went outside in the sight of everyone. They were awestruck; all gave praise to God, saying, 'We have never seen anything like this!'

Mark 2:1-12

Another woman, sick for many years knew that if she but touched the hem of His garment she would be cured:

As they were going, a woman who had suffered from hemor-rhages for twelve years came up behind him and touched the tassel on his cloak. 'If only I can touch his cloak,' she thought, 'I shall get well.' Jesus turned around and saw her and said, 'Courage, daughter! Your faith has restored you to health.'

Matthew 9:20-22

Proof that this sacrament has special powers is evident when Christ reacts to power going out from Him even when He did not see the woman whose faith brought it forth. Faith is the key to receiving this sacrament worthily.

When he had finished this discourse in the hearing of the people, he entered Capernaum. A centurion had a servant he held in high regard, who was at that moment sick to the point of death. When he heard about Jesus he sent some Jewish elders to him, asking him to come and save the life of his servant. Upon approaching Jesus they petitioned him earnestly. 'He deserves this favor from you,' they said, 'because he loves our people, and even built our synagogue for us.' Jesus set out with them. When he was only a short distance from the house, the centurion sent friends to tell him: 'Sir, do not trouble yourself, for I am not worthy to have you enter my house. That is why I did not presume to come to you myself. Just give the order and my servant will be cured. I too am a man who knows the meaning of an order, having soldiers under my command. I say to one, "On your way," and off he goes: to another, "Come here," and he comes; to my slave, "Do this," and he does it' Jesus showed amazement on hearing this, and turned to the crowd which was following him to say, 'I tell you, I have never found so much faith among the Israelites.' When the deputation returned to the house, they found the servant in perfect health.

Luke 7:1-10

Just as the Centurion recognized that Christ had servants who would do his bidding and that He could bestow His power on them, we must realize that Christ has bestowed His healing power to His ministers on earth and that they can exercise these powers in this sacrament.

They expelled many demons, anointed the sick with oil, and worked many cures.

Mark 6:13

The healing power of Christ has been passed down from generation to generation from Christ to His apostles and from them to His ministers in His Church. St. James, His apostle, tells us in the Church how to receive this sacrament.

If anyone among you is suffering hardship, he must pray. If a person is in good spirits, he should sing a hymn of praise. Is there anyone sick among you? He should ask for the presbyters of the church. They in turn are to pray over him, anointing him with oil in the Name [of the Lord.] This prayer uttered in faith will reclaim the one who is ill, and the Lord will restore him to health. If he has committed any sins, forgiveness will be his.Hence, declare your sins to one another, and pray for one another, that you may find healing.

James 5:13-16

So, the sick within the Church are especially blessed with this healing sacrament. As the people of God we have rights and obligations to bring our sick to His ministers so that they can pray over them with us and anoint their bodies with sacred oil. We do not have to be afraid that receiving this sacrament means that the sick person will die. Rather, we can hope that both body and soul will be healed.

THIS SACRAMENT MAY BE RECEIVED MORE THAN ONCE.

The sacrament of Anointing of the Sick is the blessing of a sick person by:

Anointing with oil;

Prayers offered for strength against despair;

Prayers offered for the restoration of spiritual health;

And the forgiveness of sins for which the person is truly sorry.

These seven sacraments, all given to us by God, are His ongoing life with us at all times. They are the means by which God is always with us and we are never abandoned by Him any time during our earthly life. The keeper and dispenser of these sacraments is His Church, acting through His priests. There is no other place on earth we can go to receive them. That is why it is so important for us to stay close to His Church.

We may hear the Word of God preached elsewhere; we may pray to Him in private or in public, but to receive His life through the sacraments He left us, we must go to His Church to receive them. We can be good without them but we will be far better with them.

Precepts of the Catholic Church

$\mathcal{A}$ precept is a rule of action or conduct. The Precepts of the Catholic Church provide SIX rules to minimally govern our conduct or behavior as members of the Church. Adherence to these six rules is the least effort of adoration and worship that we can make to Christ in return for the love He has shown to us in giving us the sacraments.

These precepts are our way of keeping the Church that Christ established vibrant and alive for its members and the generations to come after us. They are the rules by which we have a **UNIFIED** way of expressing to God our love for Him. He deserves this from us as a community of people – not individuals. Through these precepts we **ACT** as a generation of people. Our spiritual lives take on meaning as a group for the sake of Christ. We are acting in unison as members of His Church.

When we take on the rights and obligations of being His people, we must be very careful of our actions and behavior with regard to these precepts. In order to realize how much regard God has for His people, read *The Song of Song's* in the Old Testament. In Christian tradition, the Song has been interpreted as the union between Christ and the Church, whom He loves tenderly and beautifully. Also St. Paul's discourse in Ephesians, Chapter 5 of the New Testament describing Christ as the head of the Church and His people as the Body. He is the savior of His people.

When these readings penetrate the eye of our hearts, we realize that we must be very careful how we treat this Bride of Christ because He will be seriously offended if we offend her. Therefore, if we take on the privilege of being confirmed in this faith, we also take on the obligation of living our lives with her precepts in mind.

The sacraments were given to us by **GOD**, and can **NEVER** be changed by man. However, the precepts of the Church were instituted by MEN, and so they can be changed by men. These precepts are:

I

TO ASSIST AT MASS ON ALL SUNDAYS (or Saturday Vigils) AND HOLY DAYS OF OBLIGATION

The first Mass was said by Christ at the Feast of the Passover that He dearly wanted to share with His apostles. At this First Mass, Christ brought a **NEW COVENANT** to mankind from God. God made other covenants with His people, e.g., Noah and Abraham. This New Covenant is greater than any other of His covenants because the new sacrifice Christ offers is His own Body and Blood for the forgiveness of sins. This happens at every Mass that is offered anywhere in the world.

The early Christians established Sunday as the day of worship to signify that this was a new covenant with a new Church of believers in the **DIVINITY OF CHRIST** through the **RESURRECTION** that took place on the first day of the week. St. Paul refers to this kind of worship in the New Testament:

> On the first day of the week when we gathered for the breaking of bread, Paul preached to them.
>
> *Acts 20:7*

Sunday was established as the seventh day of worship in honor of Christ's Resurrection on Easter. It is the holiest of all the Holy Days. It also distinguished the followers of Christ from their Jewish brethren who kept their Sabbath on Saturday. Did you ever wonder why we have these two particular days of the week off from most work? This is the reason. Christians worship God on Sundays and Jews worship God on Saturdays.

Those who love Christ treasure the Mass and will renew this covenant with Him at least on all Sundays and the other **SIX HOLY DAYS OF OBLIGATION** which are feasts set aside by the Church as so important as to demand our attention and attendance at their celebration. The six Holy Days are:

December 8
Feast of the Immaculate Conception

This feast is celebrated in honor of Mary who was conceived in the womb of St. Anne, her mother, without original sin by a special grace from God designed to make her suitable to be a mother for Christ. The Church teaches that this doctrine was originally entrusted to the apostles and transmitted to the Church by them. After many centuries of controversial theological discussion, Pope Pius IX declared this doctrine dogma in 1854 and explained his action in an encyclical letter. In so doing he stated that:

"**...the doctrine which holds that the Most Blessed Virgin Mary was preserved from all stain of original sin in the first instant of her conception, by a singular grace and privilege of Almighty God, in consideration of the merits of Jesus Christ, savior of the human race, has been revealed by God and must, therefore, firmly and constantly be believed by all the faithful.**"

December 25
CHRISTMAS DAY

This feast celebrates the birth of Jesus Christ, Son of God, into this world. He was born of the Virgin Mary in a stable in Bethlehem with Joseph, His foster-father present at His birth.

January 1
FEAST OF MARY, MOTHER OF GOD

This feast used to be called the Feast of the Circumcision. Mary brought Jesus to the temple in accordance with the law and the covenant God had made with Abraham that all males should be circumcised to set them apart as His chosen people and their acceptance of Him as their God. (Genesis 17:10-11) Most significantly, Simeon, who had been promised by God that he would not die until he saw the promised Messiah was in the temple when Mary and Joseph brought Jesus there and Simeon recognized this infant as the Messiah. (Luke 2:25)

ASCENSION THURSDAY
FORTY DAYS AFTER EASTER

This feast celebrates the Ascension of Christ into heaven forty days after His Resurrection on Easter Sunday. It falls on the Thursday after the Sixth Sunday of Easter. Jesus spent forty days after His Resurrection from death walking, talking and eating with His apostles to prove to them and to the world that He had conquered death for all of us. (Acts 1:1-9)

AUGUST 15
ASSUMPTION OF THE BLESSED
VIRGIN MARY INTO HEAVEN

This feast celebrates the assumption of Mary, both body and soul, into heaven after her death. It is only fitting that the body of Mary, born without original sin on her soul, should not suffer the decay of death. It is another example of Christ's love for this beautiful woman, His mother.

The Assumption of Mary into heaven was the traditional teaching of the Church Fathers from earliest times. In the year 1950, Pope Pius XII declared this doctrine to be infallible and must be believed by all the faithful.

NOVEMBER 1
ALL SAINTS DAY

This feast celebrates the Feast Day of all those who have died and are in heaven with God, but for whom no special day has been set aside. Someday this will be our Feast Day, too!

II

TO FAST AND ABSTAIN
ON DAYS APPOINTED
BY LEADERS OF THE FAITHFUL

This precept, more than any other, demonstrates the changes that may take place from time to time regarding Church laws made by man. Days of fast and abstinence have been changed many times, but this practice of fasting from food and abstaining from meat has been an approved way of doing penance from early Biblical times.

Our Lord practiced fasting and abstaining (see Matthew 4:1-11) and in doing so approved this tradition for us too. It is supposed to help us bring our minds and hearts toward God. The season of Lent has been particularly chosen for fasting and abstaining from meat as it falls during the forty days before Easter.

Any difficulty that this precept may impart on an individual can be discussed with a priest in the confessional and the person can be relieved of this obligation by the priest if sufficient reason exists to do so.

The Lenten regulations at this time are:

ABSTINENCE:

Catholics 14 years of age and older are to abstain from eating meat on Good Friday and on all of the Fridays of Lent.

FASTING:

Catholics 18 years of age but not yet 59 years are to fast on Ash Wednesday and Good Friday. Those who are bound by this Lenten rule may take one full meal. Two smaller ones are permitted if necessary to maintain strength according to one's needs. Eating solid foods between meals is not permitted.

The law of fasting also applies to the time before receiving Holy Communion. Catholics are to abstain from food and liquids, except water, for **ONE HOUR** before receiving the Eucharist.

III

TO CONFESS OUR SINS
AT LEAST ONCE A YEAR

This precept sets forth the most minimal action to be taken by a believing Catholic in the sacrament of Penance. (John 20:23) Those who are truly confirmed Catholics will partake of it far more often. Within the Church this is often spoken of as "fulfilling your Easter Duty." The Church has set aside a time when, if you have not been to confession since the previous Easter season, then you must, in order to maintain your membership in the Church, go to confession. The time set aside for fulfilling this obligation is from Ash Wednesday to Trinity Sunday. In the Church Calendar Trinity Sunday is eight weeks after Easter Sunday.

IV

TO RECEIVE HOLY COMMUNION DURING EASTERTIME

Easter is the most important feast of the Catholic Church and has been chosen as the time for minimal profession of faith in the sacrament of the Eucharist as well as confession. These two precepts of the Church make a minimum standard for expressing a desire to maintain membership in the Church.

Those who truly believe in the Eucharist as the Body and Blood of Christ will come to Him far more often for the saving grace that comes with frequent reception of this sacrament. Also, it is an expression to others of our belief in Christ's real presence in this sacrament.

V

TO CONTRIBUTE TO THE SUPPORT OF THE CHURCH

The Church consists of the people of God. They need a house in which to gather as a community to worship Him. Therefore, they must maintain buildings for this purpose. The priests who administer the sacraments must also depend on the generosity of the people to maintain themselves and the houses of worship over which they have charge.

Catholics who understand the awesome importance of the Church will want to help in the financial needs of supporting the Church. Weekly contribution envelopes are available in most Churches and should be used by the faithful. Your priest needs to know that he is appreciated for the work that he does and he will want to maintain the house of worship in his parish in good condition.

Financial support alone is not enough. God needs many hands to do His work and time contributed to the many needs of the Church should be part of our gift to God. **PRAYER** is one of the most effective means of support for the Church. Prayer, especially for the priests who serve God, is also an essential element in support of the Church.

Each person must judge for himself the nature and the amount of support he can render to God through the Church for what God gives to him or her.

VI

TO OBSERVE THE LAWS OF THE CHURCH CONCERNING MARRIAGE

To be a member of the Church we must recognize the special nature of sacramental marriage and seek the special graces that are offered. They will be needed in order to live the kind of sacrificial life sacramental marriage demands. We can only get this special grace by going to God's priest and asking for it.

This precept requires us to defend our belief in sacramental marriage in a world where this kind of marriage may be rejected by a great many people. It means that as Catholics we cannot participate in marriage ceremonies that involve confirmed Catholics who are not asking the blessing of God and His Church in their marriage ceremony. Sometimes this is a very hard precept to keep. If we do participate in this kind of ceremony, we are conveying the belief that God's blessing is not important.

It is easy to succumb to the temptation to attend such marriage ceremonies because they involve people we love and we do not want to hurt their feelings. But if we do attend them, it is God's feelings that will be hurt the most. It is another way we can affirm our love for Him by keeping this precept of His Church. If our confirmed friends truly understand their faith, then they will not be offended if you do not attend such a ceremony because they will know the reason why. If they do not understand the faith, then it should be explained to them.

Most important though is the fact that if we decide to marry, we will go to the priest and ask for God's blessing on our marriage. If we do not do this, it is a grave insult to our God. Children will probably result from marriage and it is important to have an understanding that the children will participate in the faith with us and receive the sacraments in their order.

The Bible

The sacred Word of God is revealed to man in the writings contained in the Bible. He is the author of all of the Books of the Bible since His inspiration caused men to write them. These books are only a part of God's relationship with man but a most significant and important part that He wanted revealed to us. His revelations to us through the Bible are perfect, that is, free from error, though imperfect humans were used to write the Divine Word.

The meaning of this Divine Word is not always clear to us and Catholics will rely on the **TEACHING AUTHORITY OF THE CHURCH** to guide them in their interpretation of Bible passages. The Catholic Church teaches that the Bible is **INFALLIBLE IN DOCTRINE** though many forms are used to affirm the truths it contains; sometimes poetry, sometimes prose, sometimes allegory, sometimes history, etc. Since the Church is the teaching authority for the Bible and the Bible is considered an infallible doctrinal authority, the Church must be considered an infallible teacher (or interpreter) of its doctrines. God would not allow His children to be deceived by erroneous teaching in matters as important as our faith and morals. Therefore, He gives to His Church the obligation of interpreting His Divine Word for His people.

The **OLD TESTAMENT** contains the revelation of God to man and His Covenants with His chosen people and their relationship with Him from the time of Creation to the time of Christ.

The **NEW TESTAMENT** contains the witness of the apostles to the **DIVINITY OF CHRIST** and the New Covenant of Christ with man.

The Church is unable to assign exact dates to the writings and events that occurred in the first eleven Chapters of the Book of Genesis. They contain the Divine revelation of Creation to the time of Abraham. History tries to link the Bible and the history of the people in it with historical fact. Abraham is the first person in the Bible with whom historians and Biblical scholars can assign a time in history. Historically, therefore, the period from Creation to Abraham cannot be proven.

Abraham, however, is an historical figure as well as a Biblical person and Biblical scholars consider that his life coincided with that of a historical Babylonian King, Hammurabi, who is believed to have lived in approximately 1947 to 1905 B.C. (Before Christ). The Bible is not concerned with history, however, and the Divine revelation is to be believed as the **WORD OF GOD**. The succeeding Books of the Old Testament also contain the revealed Word of God to mankind through the events in the lives of His chosen people from Abraham to the time of the coming of the Messiah, Jesus Christ.

There are **FORTY-SIX BOOKS** in the **OLD TESTAMENT**. Protestant and Jewish Bibles do not include the Books of Tobit, Judith, Wisdom, Ecclesiasticus, Baruch, and the two Books of Maccabees. Also parts of Daniel and Esther are excluded. Protestant and Jewish Biblical scholars do not believe these excluded works to be the inspired Word of God and are, therefore, not included in their versions of the Bible.

The **NEW TESTAMENT** contains **TWENTY-FIVE BOOKS.** Their inspired writings were those of the original Hebrew, Aramaic and Greek texts. Translations do not have the very words of the inspired writings but the

Catholic Church has kept the translations free from doctrinal error and as true to the original texts as is possible.
The sacredness and reverence for God's Word is an awesome responsibility that the Church realizes and keeps in
mind in her translations and teachings. None of the writings of the New Testament occurred while Christ was still
on earth. All were completed by around the year 100 A.D
(anno Domini or after Divinity).

When we attend Mass the gospel is an important part of
this ritual. Just before the gospel is read, the Catholics in
the congregation make a sign of affirmation in the sacred
Word of God. They do this by placing the thumb of the
right hand on the FOREHEAD and making the Sign of the
Cross as a sign that they believe the gospel with their
minds.

They then place the thumb on their LIPS and make the
Sign of the Cross as a sign that they will speak the gospel
with their mouths.

They then place the thumb on their HEARTS and make
the Sign of the Cross as a sign they will keep the gospel
in their hearts.

Reading the Bible, both the Old and New Testaments, is
essential to a full and appreciative understanding of
God's relationship with man. There is an inspiration that
comes through the actual reading of God's Word that can
be achieved in no other way. For the mature Catholic to
appreciate and practice his faith in a meaningful way,
personal reading of the Divine Word is an absolute
necessity. God speaks in a special way to those who read
His Word.

Catholic Bibles will always have an Imprimatur by a
Bishop or Cardinal in the front section of the Bible.
Protestants usually rely on the St. James Version of the
Bible. It is not a Catholic Bible.

The Teaching Authority of the Church

There is a constant, on-going revelation of Divine truth from the Holy Spirit to the Church. The Church is the place where this knowledge, this truth is deposited and made available to its members. The Holy Spirit is always active, making this Divine revelation to all generations. The Word of God is the written revelation of truth given by Him to men He inspired to make it available to all of us. It is so important in our lives that Christ established a church with men chosen by Him to interpret His Word for us. He does so to protect all of us from erroneous beliefs that may seriously affect our lives in an evil way.

Therefore, we are obliged to believe in the INFALLIBLE TEACHING AUTHORITY OF THE CHURCH in matters of FAITH AND MORALS. These teachings come to us through the Pope who is the head of the Church and the universal shepherd of Christ's faithful flock. It is a rare occurrence for any teaching to be declared an infallible one. The Pope speaks ex cathedra, (from the chair of Peter, as visible head of the church), when this happens and only two times in the last two centuries has this happened:

In 1854 when Pius IX declared that the long held tradition of the Church that Mary was conceived in the womb of St. Anne without the stain of original sin on her soul is true. It is called the Immaculate Conception and is now an infallible doctrine of the Church.

In 1950 when Pius XII declared that another long held tradition of the Church that Mary was bodily assumed into Heaven is true. It is called the Assumption of Mary into Heaven and is now an infallible doctrine of the Church.

The truths of our faith are revealed to us in several ways:

By God the Father directly;

By Christ through His teachings and instruction of the apostles;

By the Bible which is the inspired Word of God;

By ordained men of God who transmit these teachings to us, guard them, and protect them from error;

By using our own reason;

By using our own conscience that has been educated to the truth.

That these truths are protected from error is a promise Christ made to His apostles:

When Jesus came to the neighborhood of Caesarea Phillippi, he asked his disciples this question: 'Who do people say that the Son of Man is?' They replied, 'Some say John the Baptizer, others Elijah, still others Jeremiah or one of the prophets.' 'And you,' he said to them, 'who do you say that I am?' 'You are the Messiah,' Simon Peter answered, 'the Son of the living God!' Jesus replied, 'Blest are you, Simon son of Jonah! No mere man has revealed this to you, but my heavenly Father. I for my part declare to you, you are 'Rock,' and on this rock I will build my church, and the jaws of death shall not prevail against it. I will entrust to you the keys of the kingdom of heaven. Whatever you declare bound on earth shall be bound in heaven; whatever you declare loosed on earth shall be loosed in heaven.' Then he strictly ordered his disciples not to tell anyone that he was the Messiah.

Matthew 16:13-20

The Popes continue the teaching of the message of salvation by interpreting the Divine Word and applying it to social problems in every generation. This is done through letters or encyclicals specifically stating the Church's teaching on any subject affecting the faith and morals of her members.

These teachings may include those doctrines that are part of the TRADITION of the Church but may not be revealed in the Divine Word. On rare occasions a Pope may declare a traditional teaching infallible doctrine. When the Pope does this the Holy Spirit intercedes with the Pope and his counselors and will prevent them from declaring such a traditional teaching an infallible doctrine if it is NOT TRUTH. So, we profess a faith in the continuing presence of the Holy Spirit in the world when we accept such a doctrine as a matter we MUST believe.

Ecumenical Councils of the Church meet to deliberate matters of religious significance to its members. These councils are a calling together by the Pope of his bishops and major prelates of the worldwide universal Church. They meet and discuss matters affecting the whole Church and bring together many minds for the solving of problems. Some of these are the correction of heretical beliefs that spring up from time to time that may lead the faithful astray and correcting abuses within the Church.

Through these councils, the bishops can formulate a UNIFIED way for the observance of Church laws. When many of God's people act as one, a strengthening of faith occurs. In the New Testament, St. Paul performs this service in his letters to the various churches he established for Christ. He often clarifies the doctrines and rebukes, inspires and praises the members of the Church to whom he is writing. He became a slave for Christ. The bishops of the councils are much like St. Paul in their efforts to help us to know, to love and to serve Christ through this beautiful Church that He loved so much that He laid down His life for her.

At the Passover Meal at the Last Supper, Christ gave a long discourse to His apostles. At the end of this discourse He said to them:

'I have told you all this
to keep your faith from being shaken.
Not only will they expel you from the synagogues;
a time will come
when anyone who puts you to death
will claim to be serving God!
All this they will do [to you]
because they knew neither the Father nor me.
But I have told you these things
that when their hour comes
you may remember my telling you of them.
I did not speak of this with you from the beginning
because I was with you.
Now that I go back to him who sent me,
not one of you asks me,
"Where are you going?"
Because I have had all this to say to you,
you are overcome with grief.
Yet I tell you the sober truth:
It is much better for you that I go.
If I fail to go,
the Paraclete will never come to you,
whereas if I go,
I will send him to you.
When he comes,
he will prove the world wrong
about sin,
about justice,
about condemnation.
About sin –
in that they refuse to believe in me;
about justice –
from the fact that I go to the Father

and you can see me no more;
about condemnation –
for the prince of this world has been condemned.
I have much more to tell you,
but you cannot bear it now.
When he comes, however,
being the Spirit of truth,
he will guide you to all truth.
He will not speak on his own,
but will speak only what he hears,
and will announce to you the things to come.
In doing this he will give glory to me,
because he will have received from me
what he will announce to you.
All that the Father has belongs to me.
That is why I said that what he will announce to you
he will have from me.
Within a short time you will lose sight of me,
but soon after that you shall see me again.'

John 16:1-16

Conclusion

You have reviewed the essentials of the Catholic faith that you must believe in order to be confirmed. As you live this faith and grow in maturity, you will discover a rich treasure of knowledge stored for you through the centuries by people who have loved God through His Church. They have left this wealth of knowledge for you to discover. It takes a lifetime to absorb even a part of it and you will be thrilled with the new discoveries you constantly make about this wonderful faith and the loving church that has kept it alive and active for you for over 2000 years.

If you leave the ceremony that confirms you as a member of the Catholic Church and believe that your religious instruction years are over, you will be making an erroneous assumption. Your religious life as an adult is just beginning! You must search the rest of your life for ways in which to enrich your life as a member of this Church. You may accomplish this through service to others and by learning more about your faith. Always show your love for God in your daily life by keeping Him uppermost in your thoughts, and the frequent reception of the sacraments, especially receiving His Body and Blood in Holy Communion.

What will it be like living a Catholic life in a modern world? Pope Paul VI told us in these words:

You are like seafarers on a stormy sea – the sea of unbelief, of irregularity, of diversity of opinion, of liberty and license given the manifestations which are contrary to your beliefs, to the Christian way of life, to God, to Christ and to the Church.

Nothing afflicts us more than to see the emergence of aggressions, snares and dangers for the firmness and salvation of our sons. Whosoever has the heart of a brother and a father, as he who the pastor of souls must, lives and suffers in a state of continuous and sincere fear...

It leads to another form of weakness, also widespread today, which at the time led poor Peter to his graver fall. He wanted to hide, to disguise himself; he wanted to conform to his environment to evade the consequences of his devotion to Christ and so he denied him.

Spoken to an audience in St. Peter's Square

Both Peter and Judas Iscariot denied Christ and they were two of the twelve God chose. The characteristics of both are in all of us. Judas did not repent of his denial and Peter did. Christ built His Church on the one who did.

And who do you think Christ is? Is He the Messiah? Is He God? Did He die on the cross for the forgiveness of sins? You cannot join this Church believing that He is just a good teacher, a good man – because He is much more than that.

It is now time for you to decide whether you will be confirmed in this faith or not. It is time for you to make a Covenant with God of your own. It is time for you to decide:

"Do I Believe In **JESUS CHRIST** as the **SON OF GOD**?"

If the answer is yes, are you ready to promise God that:

I know and believe the Nicene and/or Apostles' Creed;

I know the Seven Sacraments;

I will make every effort to keep the Six Precepts of the Church;

I know the Ten Commandments and will base my life on them;

I will pray for others both in and out of the Church;

I will help others to the best of my ability;

I realize that my life hereafter is a witness for Christ;

I realize that I will give glory or scandal to Him by the way I live my life;

I will learn as much as I can about Christ, His Church and His teachings the rest of my life;

I will have compassion for all people in and out of the Church, realizing that they are human, just as I am, and may fail from time to time in their efforts to lead a Christian life;

I will refrain from calling others hypocrites whether they go to Church or not because I do not know why they act in the manner they do;

I will defend my faith at all times under all circumstances.

If you can promise God all these things then you can say, **"I spoke your testimonies and I was not ashamed," just as St. Paul did.**

From this time forward you will experience a special knowledge of what it means to have faith and to use it.

The coming of the Holy Spirit to you is a miraculous event. The apostles experienced it this way:

When the day of Pentecost came it found them gathered in one place. Suddenly from up in the sky there came a noise like a strong, driving wind which was heard all through the house where they were seated. Tongues as of fire appeared which parted and came to rest on each of them. All were filled with the Holy Spirit. They began to express themselves in foreign tongues and make bold proclamation as the Spirit prompted them.

Staying in Jerusalem at the time were devout Jews of every nation under heaven. These heard the sound, and assembled in a large crowd. They were much confused because each one heard these men speaking his own language. The whole occurrence astonished them. They asked in utter amazement, 'Are not all of these men who are speaking Galileans? How is that each of us hears them in his native tongue? We are Parthians, Medes, and Elamites. We live in Mesopotamia, Judea and Cappadocia, Pontus, the province of Asia, Phrygia and Pamphylia, Egypt, and the regions of Libya around Cyrene. There are even visitors from Rome – all Jews, or those who have come over to Judaism; Cretans and Arabs, too. Yet each of us hears them speaking in his own tongue about the marvels God has accomplished.' They were dumbfounded, and could make nothing at all of what had happened.

'What does this mean?' they asked one another, while a few remarked with a sneer, 'They have had too much new wine!'

Peter stood up with the Eleven, raised his voice, and addressed them: 'You who are Jews, indeed all of you staying in Jerusalem! Listen to what I have to say. You must realize that these men are not drunk, as you seem to think. It is only nine in the morning! No, it is what Joel the prophet spoke of:

'It shall come to pass in the last days, says God,
that I will pour out a portion of my spirit on all mankind:

Your sons and daughters shall prophesy,
your young men shall see visions
and your old men shall dream dreams.
Yes, even on my servants and handmaids
I will pour out a portion of my spirit in those days,
and they shall prophesy.
I will work wonders in the heavens above
And signs on the earth below:
blood, fire, and a cloud of smoke.

The sun shall be turned to darkness and the moon to blood
before the coming of that great and glorious day of the Lord.
Then shall everyone be saved who calls on the name of the
Lord.

'Men of Israel, listen to me! Jesus the Nazorean was a man
whom God sent to you with miracles, wonders, and signs as
his credentials. These God worked through him in your midst,
as you well know. He was delivered up by the set purpose
and plan of God; you even made use of pagans to crucify and
kill him. God freed him from death's bitter pangs, however,
and raised him up again, for it was impossible that death
should keep its hold on him: David says of him:

"I have set the Lord ever before me,
with him at my right hand I shall not be disturbed.
My heart has been glad and my tongue has rejoiced,
my body will live on in hope,
for you will not abandon my soul to the nether world,
nor will you suffer your faithful one to undergo corruption.
You have shown me the paths of life;
you will fill me with joy in your presence."

'Brothers, I can speak confidently to you about our father
David. He died and was buried, and his grave is in our midst
to this day. He was a prophet and knew that God had sworn
to him that one of his descendants would sit upon his throne.
He said that he was not abandoned to the nether world, nor
did his body undergo corruption, thus proclaiming beforehand
the resurrection of the Messiah. This is the Jesus God has

raised up, and we are his witnesses. Exalted at God's right
hand, he first received the promised Holy Spirit from the
Father, then poured this Spirit out on us. This is what you
now see and hear. David did not go up to heaven, yet David
says,

'The Lord said to my Lord,
Sit at my right hand
until I make your enemies your footstool.'
Therefore, let the whole house of Israel know beyond any
doubt that God has made both Lord and Messiah this Jesus
whom you crucified.'

When they heard this, they were deeply shaken. They asked
Peter and the other apostles, 'What are we to do, brothers?'
Peter answered: 'You must reform and be baptised, each one
of you, in the name of Jesus Christ, that your sins may be forgiven; then you will receive the gift of the Holy Spirit. It was to
you and your children that the promise was made, and to all
those still far off whom the Lord our God calls.'

In support of his testimony he used many other arguments,
and kept urging, 'Save yourselves from this generation which
has gone astray.' Those who accepted his message were
baptized; some three thousand were added that day.

                                                           Acts 2:1-40

The descent of the Holy Spirit on the apostles that day
was the birth of the living Church. As a member of this
Church, I want to welcome you to the Catholic faith. It is
a difficult life but a most rewarding one. You are now the
inheritor of the greatest treasure on earth. St. Paul told
the early Christians how to live this life when he was a
prisoner in Rome:

But I am not ashamed, for I know him in whom I have
believed, and I am confident that he is able to guard what has

been entrusted to me until that Day.

Take as a model of sound teaching what you have heard me say, in faith and love in Christ Jesus. Guard the rich deposit of faith with the help of the Holy Spirit who dwells within us.

2 Timothy 1:12-14

If you are steadfast in this faith, like St. Paul, you will receive the reward of life eternal with God forever. He made you in His image and likeness and wants your love. Give it to Him and you will know peace of mind and soul in your life on the earth and then be happy with Him in eternity forever.

If you are to lead a truly Catholic life, the decision to be confirmed in this faith must be a personal one that you make for yourself. No one can make it for you. If you do decide to be confirmed, then I welcome you as a fellow Catholic into the rich deposit of faith that is the Catholic Church. You will now see life in a different way from others who do not believe that Christ is the Son of God.

Christ asked a young man whose sight he had restored:

'Do you believe in the Son of Man?' He answered, 'Who is he, sir, that I may believe in him?' 'You have seen him,' Jesus replied. 'He is speaking to you now.' ['I do believe, Lord,' he said, and bowed down to worship him. Then Jesus said:]

'I came into this world to divide it,
to make the sightless see
and the seeing blind.'

John 9:35-39

If you practice this faith you will no longer see only with your eyes but with your soul as well. There is a most magnificent treasure that has been left for you as an inheritance while you live on earth. This treasure is the truth that we all yearn to know. It is here for you to discover, to believe, and to love. But never forget that it will divide you from the world that lives without spiritual sight. You will now live *in* the world but not be *of* the world.

Always keep this book as a reminder of the decision you made and the reasons why you made it. By living this faith you will come to know a peace in your life that others cannot understand, especially when your cross sometimes seems too heavy to bear.

May God bless you and yours,

Barbara Del Buono

ABOUT THE AUTHOR

Barbara Del Buono is a convert to the Roman Catholic faith. She grew up in Oklahoma, when that state was considered Catholic mission territory. She did not know the Catholic Church existed until she was in high school.

Barbara's introduction to Catholicism was through her employer, C. Robert Ingram. He arranged for her to take instructions in the faith from Monsignor John Mason Connor, Rector of Our Lady of Perpetual Help Cathedral in Oklahoma City. The nine months Barbara spent being privately instructed by him are still cherished by her today. Many of the concepts in this book are the result of his excellent teaching. Barbara believes it is necessary for each person to *learn* the essential beliefs of the Catholic faith, *believe* that these are truth, and *practice* them in daily life.

At the age of twenty, in spite of her family's objections, she chose to be baptized by Monsignor Connor on December 25, 1948. Barbara considers her decision to become a Catholic the most important decision of her life. Robert and Bertha Ingram became her godparents and excellent examples in the faith.

Monsignor Connor officiated at the marriage of Barbara to a young law school student at the University of Oklahoma, John Del Buono, on January 27, 1950 at the Cathedral. Their wedding reception was held at the home of Robert and Bertha Ingram. Barbara and John moved to Connecticut where John has practiced law since 1955. They have eight children, thirteen grandchildren and six great-grandchildren. Barbara and John celebrated their 50th wedding anniversary on January 27, 2000.

Barbara taught Confraternity of Christian Doctrine classes and was president of the Home-School Association of the Catholic grammar school attended by all eight of her children. She believes that parents are the primary teachers of religion to their children. Barbara wrote this book to help guide parents in this endeavor. It is a supplement that enhances CCD classes and unites the parent and child with the efforts made to increase the knowledge of the faith being imparted by both the family and the Church.

CPSIA information can be obtained at www.ICGtesting.com
Printed in the USA
BVOW07s1017111114

374593BV00001B/150/P